STOI
Y2K MADNESS!

STOP THE Y2K MADNESS!

EXPOSING THE PURVEYORS OF PANIC

by William J. Murray
and
Robert Armstrong

Copy Editor – Nancy M. Murray

William J. Murray
Robert Armstrong
906 Lafayette Blvd
Fredericksburg, VA 22404
(540) 370-4200

STOP THE Y2K MADNESS
Copyright 1999 William J. Murray & Robert Armstrong

Published by:
MFM Publishing, P.O. Box 7416
Fredericksburg, VA 22404
(540) 370-4200

ISBN 0-940917-04-1

Printed in the United States of America

CONTENTS

FORWARD: *Anarchy in the Streets* 7

CHAPTER ONE: *The Real Y2K Problem: A Self-Fulfilling Prophecy* 13

CHAPTER TWO: *Our Computer Society: Examining the Two-Digit Problem* 33

CHAPTER THREE: *Y2K Armageddon: Apocalyptic Bandwagon of "Hype"* 45

CHAPTER FOUR: *Exposing the Prophets (Profits) of Doom and Gloom* 63

CHAPTER FIVE: *Profiteers and Hucksters: Put Them Out of Business!* 81

CHAPTER SIX: *Pain and Death Caused by Misperceptions, NOT Computers* 103

CHAPTER SEVEN: *The Y2K Problem Is Being Overcome* 119

CHAPTER EIGHT: *Y2K May Even Have Some Benefits* 145

CHAPTER NINE: *Practical Preparation: Finding a Proper Balance* 159

FORWARD

ANARCHY IN THE STREETS!

"Get ready to ring in the last year of the 20th Century!" the voice blared on the television set, as millions around the world watched the milling throng in Times Square. "Thirty seconds!"

The crowd was already in a frenzy.

Champagne shortages told the story.

After all, this was the last day of the millennium, and that only happens every thousand years.

Mass hysteria gripped segments of the population as the countdown continued.

"Fifteen seconds and counting......"

The announcer told the verdict, but few could hear over the screams and shouts!

Sinister criminal elements stood poised for action, waiting for the magic moment.

Some Christians prayed.

Survivalist commune dwellers tried to relax, somehow believing that their decision to join a new sub-culture would lead to their peace and prosperity.

Y2K "doomsayers" cringed as they awaited the supposed fate of the nation and world.

"Ten . . . nine . . eight . . . seven . . . "

Champagne glasses tilted. Corks popped. Motorcycle engines roared. Hopeless romantics embraced. Outright screaming rose from the New York City skyline.

"Six . . . five . . . four . . . "

Police forces braced for the probable chaos. Even the police horses sensed something foreboding in the cold, midnight air.

The brand new, specially made Waterford crystal ball entered the final stage of its historic drop.

Some computer owners turned off their machines, sure that they would fail anyway at the stroke of midnight. Survivalists smiled, confident that the thousands of dollars' worth of dried food products they had purchased would get them through the coming storm. A good number of spiritual prophets, computer gurus and gold coin dealers were sound asleep. After all, they had already made their "Y2K money" and would celebrate by looking at their bank accounts in the morning.

"Three . . . two . . . one . . . "

"Happy New Year—-the year 2,000!"

Various global celebrations were now in high gear. Many people had waited for this precise moment for months to celebrate the passing of the old and bringing in of the new. But others had different plans. They had been making a "different" preparation for the New Year.

These "others" had been plotting their devious dealings for weeks. Young thugs suddenly began to be bold in their careless disrespect for the law. These ignorant (and also panicked) individuals recklessly believed that police computers and police radios would not work, starting at midnight. They actually expected all the lights in the city to go dim at midnight making their enterprise easy.

After all, they had heard about the impending problems all year long through the mouthpieces of the Y2K doomsayers. Even well known preachers had promised that the lights, computers and even police radios would not work in the year 2000.

Y2K. This self-fulfilling prophecy had already netted some people many millions of dollars, while others were huddling in makeshift wilderness cabins or in caves eagerly adding hot sauce to the tasteless dried food they had purchased in buckets.

The predicted "doomsday" had arrived!

Levelheaded, balanced people were "laying low" while other people panicked. Opportunists, a few television evangelists, authors, coin dealers and all those who had preyed on the fearful and gullible about the Y2K saga of End Time events, watched their television sets to see how wrong or right they would be. Even though they were wrong, it was too late to stop the events they had set in motion.

Chaos began to swirl through the nation's big cities.

Looting. Rioting. Fires. Breaking and entering. Stabbings. Shootings.

"Let's empty out this store," a young man yelled to his gang brother on 42nd Street. Nobody was going to stop them; after all, nobody could. The Y2K bug had shut down all the police radios and computers, or so they believed.

The mayhem of the Y2K would cause disruptions beyond belief. "How would the police have time to come after me?" the young man thought. "They will have more important stuff to do," he mused with a smile to himself. Before daybreak, he would be one of the few people "on the plus side" of things—-provided he didn't get caught. He bashed in the window of the electronics store with his tire iron.

The lights had not yet gone out as predicted by those he had read on the Internet, but he was sure it would happen any minute. As the glass crashed to the ground the unexpected happened; the store alarm went off. "It doesn't matter", he thought, "The phones are down, the police won't respond."

Then what he didn't expect happened. Others were following him into the store. There was mayhem as young men grabbed for the valuable electronic goods. Police cars could be heard not far off. Someone set a fire in the store; the young man did not know who.

When the police arrived, the looters coming out of the stores on 42nd Street outnumbered them. The looters were shocked to see cops. The lights went off as the flames from the stores severed power lines. Shots rang out as the police tried to hold the line. In the street the young man lay bleeding. "My God," he thought, "what if the computers and phones don't work, what if the radios don't work and they can't send an ambulance?"

What caused this anarchy?

How in the world could a simple two-digit computer program from the mid-1950's cause such widespread devastation?

The doomsayers were wrong. The police radios did work. Police did respond in their riot gear. Power was eventually restored as the lines brought down by the fires were repaired. The stock market opened on January 3, 2000 with insurance company stocks down and construction company stocks up. The electricity was on and the computers were working. Some were very embarrassed by how they had been deceived by the doomsayers. The young man who broke into the electronics store on 42nd Street was dead.

Who was at fault for the chaos on New Year's Eve? Was it the programmers in the 1950s?

No.

Were the culprits the fear mongers who had made enormous amounts of money selling Y2K as a doomsday event?

Absolutely!

The Y2K problem, with all its death and destruction, was a direct result of "purveyors of panic" whose prophets interested in profits caused calamity and catastrophe through their "bandwagon of hype."

Blood is on their hands as they count their millions!

Let's examine and EXPOSE this Y2K Armageddon for what it REALLY is...

The Real
Y2K Problem:

---

*A Self-Fulfilling
Prophecy*

CHAPTER 1

Our hearts sank when we read that yet another well-known evangelical leader had jumped on the Y2K panic bandwagon. With so many preachers promoting a Y2K Armageddon, social unrest is now almost a certainty. There will probably be looting and disorder in some big cities, and people may die.

None of the disorder, none of the chaos, not a single death will be caused by a computer failure.

Sadly, the coming disaster will be caused by the greed of those who are making millions of dollars from the fears of the people during 1999, and by politicians seeking power over the minds of men.

The purpose of this book is exactly as the title reads: *Stop The Y2K Madness!* Madness has evolved from the panic that is already gripping segments of the nation. The authors don't suffer from madness, but we are mad! We are mad at those who are spreading misinformation for profit.

We only wish we had gotten mad long ago and done more to stop the purveyors of doom sooner.

Unfortunately, most people now have their minds made up one way or the other about Y2K. Those who stir up false alarm have already done their damage to large segments of our society. Fear has already swept through the hearts of many Americans and even spread to other nations. Worldwide, many Christians are stockpiling supplies of food and fuel out of fear that has been caused by devious hucksters who have visited their churches. Non-Christians have been sold the same Y2K scenario via the Internet by dried food peddlers and gold coin dealers.

We are not burying our heads in the sand and pretending there will be no problems because of the computer glitch called Y2K. Through exhaustive research and interviewing hundreds of experts we have come to the conclusion that there will be some problems; however most of those problems will be caused not by computers but by media misinformation and fearful misconceptions about Y2K.

It is our intention to be balanced. It is not our intent to demean any person or organization, but we must be truthful in naming those who are leading the charge into the proverbial valley of death.

These alarmists will be proved wrong in these pages as well as on January 1, 2000.

Some of our personal friends are on the wrong side when it comes to Y2K preparations. Some are predicting scenarios of mass starvation and general carnage. We do not think this whole Y2K scare will help the cause of Christ, as it will only make Christians look foolish when these prophecies do not come to pass. We do not believe these prophecies have a sound biblical basis.

Oddly, the president of a large Christian television network sparked the idea for this book. One of the authors was paid to do the research for the preparation of a guide to be used as a give-away during a Y2K television special the network proposed. That TV special would have promoted a worldwide disaster scenario for Y2K.

After thorough research in 1998, he told the network president that Y2K would not cause major technical problems, that there would be no widespread collapse of the power grid or interruption in the delivery of food or water. Because he did not have the proper conclusion to fit the TV special, he was removed from the project.

Since then the daily volumes of research data have confirmed our initial appraisal. Great strides have been made to correct the Y2K computer glitch. By the end of 1999 there will be no major problems that will affect the lives or the property of Americans.

In spite of what some journalists, preachers, and computer "experts" say, the Y2K problem will be solved in virtually all critical areas and in most non-critical areas as well. The payroll system of a power company is not a critical area. Companies can have non-critical areas that are not Y2K compliant and still supply goods and services.

Noted Christian psychologist, Dr. Benjamin Keyes, says, "In this country (America), we have a handful of leaders that are creating mass hysteria. They are creating a panic. They are creating an issue (Y2K) to generate their own agendas, whether that is to sell books, tapes, or to profit some way from Y2K.... They are focused on this problem. They give a feeling that they are 'right there' with their people through thick and thin; when there is really no issue at hand!"[1]

God does not change His plan for man. He is the same yesterday, today and tomorrow. The End Times are spelled out in the Word of God. The current situation with Y2K probably has nothing to do with the plan God has for his people.

> *"Be still; and know that I am God!"*
> — *Psalm 46:10*

We do not believe a calamitous widespread disaster caused by Y2K is biblical because it would contradict Jesus' teachings about the End Times in the Gospel of Luke. Talking about the time when he will come for his church, the Lord says:

> And as it was in the days of Noah, so shall it
> be also in the days of the Son of man. They
> did eat, they drank, they married wives, they
> were given in marriage, until the day that
> Noah entered into the ark and the flood
> came and destroyed them all.
>
> Likewise also as it was in the days of Lot;
> they did eat, they drank, they bought, they
> sold, they planted, they builded; but the
> same day that Lot went out of Sodom it
> rained fire and brimstone from heaven, and
> destroyed them all.
>
> Even thus shall it be in the day when the Son
> on man is revealed.... I tell you, in that night
> there shall be two men in one bed; the one
> shall be taken, and the other shall be left. Two
> women shall be grinding together; the one
> shall be taken, and the other left. Two men
> shall be in the field; the one shall be taken and
> the other left. (Luke 17:26-30, 34-36)

From this passage, and from Revelation, it becomes
apparent that the great famines and disasters which will

shake the earth come during the Tribulation, after the taking away of the church (which is commonly referred to as the Rapture). Right up until the time of the Rapture, things will be as they were in the days of Noah and in the days of Lot-that is, days of peace and prosperity. People will be busy in their pursuit of wealth and pleasure, as is certainly true today. We also know that those were times of great wickedness, and so it will be at the Rapture.

Some of those proclaiming Y2K as the End Time are declaring that it will usher in the Second Coming of Christ. In the past others have pointed to a certain event and told their followers this indicated the Second Coming. No one knows that hour when Christ will return to this earth. December 31, 1999 is just as probable as tomorrow for His return. There is no magic date we can count on for the Second Coming.

God's judgment was a complete surprise to the spiritually dead people of Noah's day and to the wicked citizens of Sodom and Gomorrah (in spite of all the warnings they had.) The same element of surprise will be true at the Rapture, for Jesus tells us in Matthew 24:44 "Therefore be ye also ready: for in such an hour as ye think not the Son of man cometh." This very statement indicates(although it cannot be known) that the Lord will not come at the change of the Millennium simply because there is now so much almost superstitious interest in prophesy, even among unbelievers. This interest is evident just by glancing at the tabloid covers in the local supermarket. It may well be that when no real problems with Y2K occur, and when there is no sign of Jesus' appearing at the change of the millennium, that people will harden their hearts even further and give no more thought to the things of God. This would seem to be right in line with what Jesus said would happen.

One secular computer guru told us, "We laughed at the television evangelists before; now, after January 1, 2000, we will really laugh at them!"

As for predicting what will happen with the Y2K problem, the authors are not "computer gurus." But we have our finger on the pulse of what technical leaders are accomplishing. We check daily with leaders of the power and computer industries. On the other hand the purveyors of doom rarely update their information. They know that if they do, they will be unable to sell their worthless books, tapes, dried food and overpriced gold coins.

Some of the most balanced Y2K conclusions have come from A.D. 2000 and Beyond, a prestigious evangelical "think tank" in Colorado Springs. The think tank is comprised of over two dozen major ministries who hired Christian computer scientists to study the Y2K problem.

Pete Holzmann is the global coordinator of the

AD2000 Interactive Task Force. He is also the CEO of the International Christian Technologists' Association. The conclusion of their six-page January 15, 1999 *Y2K Executive Summary* states:

> *"There is no reason to panic.*
>
> *"Power grids will not shut down. Financial markets will not crash. Airplanes will continue to fly. God is still in command...*
>
> *"The real Y2K danger is not technical, but societal. If public panic arises, the doomsayers will have won."* [2]

Many Christian leaders have been pushed over the Y2K edge by those whose only motive is profit. A blind eye has been turned to those who have a real understanding of the problem at hand. Projects such as A.D 2000 And Beyond are ignored in favor of those who seek to sell church members overpriced dried food. A subject as important as Y2K must be researched completely and the information obtained must be updated constantly.

When civilization does not collapse as predicted by many TV evangelists, Christians will be looked at with disdain. Many of the lost will not accept our claims of what Christ can do in their lives when they see us looking so foolish. More harm than good will be done to the body of Christ by those who claim they are just sounding the alarm.

The alarmists in the pulpits should at least give the people correct updates on what the scientific world is doing about Y2K.

America is not perfect. Our leadership and our political structure have recently suffered severe damage through a string of scandals. However, this is still a country of creativity, hard work and ingenuity.

America is known for its commercial creativity. Quite frankly, the Y2K problem comes down to a five-letter word, M-O-N-E-Y!!

The Y2K problem may force some companies to update their computer systems and become more efficient. Achieving Y2K computer compliance before the turn of the millennium is essential for business survival.

Corporations exist for one purpose, to make a profit! Neither hurricanes, tornadoes, fires, earthquakes nor Y2K are going to stand in the way of Ford, Sony, or Exxon making a profit!

According to a study by Cap Gemini America, a Y2K services firm, "If business partnerships are like marriages, the Year 2000 problem is fast becoming grounds for divorce. Failure to achieve Y2K compliance could send many business partners out the door in the next few months—-even in the next few weeks—-as an increasing number of companies end relationships with longtime suppliers and online trading partners."[3]

The Cap Gemini America report quotes David Babler, staff engineer at AG Communication Systems, a $400 million telecommunications equipment manufacturer owned jointly by Lucent Technologies and GTE, as saying, "We are planning on dropping suppliers that are not going to be Y2K-ready, (particularly) suppliers that provide the critical equipment that we need in our product." [4]

Some suppliers already are losing contracts because of their lack of Y2K readiness, according to consultants that work on the problem. This will only spur them to great efforts, since they must be Y2K compliant to survive.

There is a tendency by some to blame Bill Gates and Microsoft for all potential Y2K problems. One of his initial comments about Y2K was, "Don't expect me to fix the world's Y2K problems. It's too big for my company to solve. Fix it yourself."[5]

No, Bill Gates can't fix all the software already in use, but he can sell new software that is Y2K compliant. His sales force is in overdrive doing just that.

Bill Gates' Microsoft is selling millions of units of Y2K compliant software to businesses who will need it.

He will make more money, not less. Also, thousands of new millionaires could emerge by helping companies solve Y2K problems for business.

Money and profits are the driving forces in coming up with Y2K answers well before the year 2000!

Corporations are in the business of making money and therefore do not want to lose the edge to their competition.

One newspaper editor told us, "All hysteria seemed to die down quickly. It seems to be simply another problem that all businesses must solve. If they don't, they don't survive. If they do, it's simply a matter of big-time, one-time maintenance costs. I guess we'll find out who procrastinated and who will lose as a result. But as far as widespread panic, forget it."[6]

Just as profit motivates most of the "doom and gloom" profiteers, profit also motivates business. Companies want to beat out their competition, especially in the Y2K compliance race.

Despite the Y2K overkill in the media, many people have not even heard of the potential computer problem, which we believe, after exhaustive research, will be no more than a few "glitches" along the way.

Thank God not every American believes the doom-sayers! In fact, an ABC News poll released on January 1, 1999 reveals that "most Americans think computer glitches expected with the arrival of the year 2000 will cause minor problems at most...

This poll shows much of the American public is aware of possible Year 2000 mistakes,' said George Strawn, director of the computer networking division of the National Science Foundation, which was a cosponsor of the poll. 'This underscores how truly integrated computers already are in our everyday lives and how much we depend on them.'" [7]

Most experts do agree that everyone should take some reasonable precautions in preparation for January 1, 2000. Although people will not starve to death or freeze to death because of Y2K, computer mistakes are still likely to occur; thus proper dissemination of Y2K information is essential.

For that reason the authors have set up an informational Internet site approaching the Y2K problem from a well-balanced perspective at http://y2k.rfcnet.org. That Internet site has received an overwhelmingly positive response.

At our Internet site discussion page, one person literate in computer software writes *"I am so glad to find others who believe as I do about Y2K. My parents have gone to the extremes, installing solar panels on the house, building a windmill, digging a well, storing dried foods and MRE's, etc. They have urged me to do the same. I have told them that I will do what I feel is prudent, but I am not willing to spend my savings account to do as they are. The sad thing is that they are not even doing this out of a Christian perspective, but rather from a New Age perspective."*

"I, like your organization, believe that the disaster of Y2K is going to be the panic. I heard that a nuclear power plant in our area is going to shut down on 12/31/99, which may be reasonable considering a "glitch" in their computer could be very bad. BUT, if this is so, hopefully they will inform the public if there will be any outages or brown outs. If there is no public information about things that are done because of a precaution, there may be panic because people assume a power outage is due to 'Y2K' instead of precaution. I have visited web sites directed to the Christian about Y2K advocating using this time as a witness for Christ to others. I hope that your cause will take the predominant view and panic can be prevented." (http://y2k.rfcnet.org)

Informed Congressional leaders tell us that "compared to people's reactions to Y2K, the computer problem itself will be negligible in its effects on people's lives."

Congressional majority leader Dick Armey said, "We should be spending more time thinking about the real anthrax threats by Osama Bin Laden or the new pinpoint missile accuracy to anywhere in Europe now available to Iran; more so than the Y2K bug!"

Y2K has been called a glitch or a Millennial "bug" or to some an apocalyptic "time bomb." To others, it is called a "hiccup," and life will go on. We believe it is a serious problem, maybe more than a "hiccup," but civilization will not end as a result of Y2K.

MANUAL OVERRIDES

There is one surety that everyone can live by: everything in the world that is run by a computer has a manual override. Those trying to sell a year's supply of dried food and a water tank to bury in one's back yard ignore this fact. Water is delivered by the force of gravity and not by a computer chip. This will be addressed in depth later.

All gas pipelines have manual valves to shut them on and off if computer chips fail, and they do fail all of the time! Gas transmission companies have chips fail in pipelines hundreds of times a year. Electric utilities have software and hardware failures thousands of times a year that sometimes stop power delivery. In all cases there are systems designed to override problems or address them manually.

The FAA's computers fail literally hundreds of times a year as well. This is why the air traffic controllers have redundant backups and manual systems to guide commercial airliners. In all critical areas there is a manual means of overcoming a computer failure. The manual overrides are there because computers fail all of the time.

In early April of 1999, the F.A.A. passed their Y2K tests without any problems. In Denver, they split all the arrivals and departures, giving one-half of them a date in the year 2000. It went off without any hitch in the programs at all.[8]

In chapter 7, we will analyze the most important industries and carefully review exactly what steps they have taken to make a smooth transition into the year 2000.

Will some or even many computers and chips fail on January 1, 2000? Yes!

Will this make a difference in how Americans live or whether families will have heat, shelter and food? No!

Most financial institutions have been Y2K compliant for years because they have had to deal with the year 2000 already. Certificates of Deposit have been issued for more than five years that have maturity dates in or past the year 2000. The bank computers handle them just fine. Major corporations and the U.S. government have been issuing bonds that come due as far away as the year 2029 and their computers manage them, buy and sell them just fine.

On March 6, 1999 the first major Y2K test of the stock market was held. More than 5,000 traders from 400 companies took part. There were no major glitches. The final test of all Wall Street systems was completed at the end of April, 1999. All systems associated with stock and bond trading worked perfectly.[9]

The authors are both members of the Board of Directors of the Religious Freedom Coalition. That organization's credit card machines were tested by our bank four years ago to make sure they were Y2K compliant. The RFC processes cards every day that have expiration dates in the year 2000 and the year 2001. Every computer in the RFC offices has been run in a mode to simulate the year 2000 and every one of them worked perfectly even though some of them are over five years old.

There are those who claim their credit and debit cards with expiration dates in 2000 and 2001 have not worked in Automated Teller Machines. It can be pointed out that not every ATM accepts cards from all banks. Was the problem the date or was the card just over the limit? The banking industry says it expects virtually no technical problems, although they do fear panic withdrawals. There is no need for people to withdraw their money from our good, strong banking system. It will remain strong, even in January, 2000.

Not a single American will starve to death because a

computer can't figure out what year it is!

But, there may still be riots and people may still die because of Y2K panic!

That panic is growing daily.

One person told us he wanted to get rid of his 1998 Mercury and buy a 20-year-old car to make sure he did not have a computer in it that would fail. He failed to realize the 20-year-old car might not run because of mechanical problems.

Others are moving out to the wilderness and drilling their own water and gas wells. Some are storing a year's worth of food.

Believe it or not, God designed wheat in such a way as to allow it to grow without a computer. It will still rain and the sun will still shine on the ground in the year 2000. God is still in control!

Well-known and respected preachers are now predicting starvation and general gloom. Entire churches are preparing for calamity. There will be calamity; the calamity will be the embarrassment caused to the Church and those of supposed faith when the world does not end on January 1, 2000.

In subsequent chapters, we will briefly look at what the doomsayers are predicting (Chapter three) and how their influence has swayed uninformed Christian leaders into parroting part of their dismay (Chapter four).

There may be financial market problems, but not because of any computer problem on Wall Street. The financial chaos could come when people take huge amounts of cash out of the bank and sell stocks because of unfounded fears. (Note: The Federal Reserve plans on printing $50 to $100 billion extra to have on hand at banks to alleviate this fear. That may not be enough!) Huge drops could come in the stock market as early as October of 1999 because of prophets of doom who are making big money selling everything from newsletters and videotapes to canned corn!

It is time to separate Y2K fact from Y2K fiction.

Our Computer Society:

Examining the Two-Digit Problem

CHAPTER 2

In order to determine how serious the Y2K threat is, we begin by looking at exactly what the problem is. Originally, it was nothing more than simply a computer problem.

William McKinley was president in 1900. He doesn't appear in many high school history books anymore, but he was the president at the turn of the past century.

When the clock ticks into the last year of this century, the year 2000, computers that are not Y2K compliant will read their data as appearing in the era of President McKinley, instead of the year 2000.

In Y2K, "Y" stands for the year, and "K" in scientific terms stands for the number 1000. Thus, Y2K is the year 2000, the last year of the twentieth century.

In the early days of computer information services, memory was very expensive, but not very compact. Most storage was done on huge magnetic tapes that slowly ran past reader heads much like a tape recorder. By asking the developers to conserve space, organizations were able to realize millions of dollars in savings.

In addition, older applications and computers were not expected to be used twenty or thirty years into the future. Computers were brand new, and only a handful of computer experts knew how to run them in the 1960's— much less predict what the future of the computers would hold.

Some, but not many, computer applications put into service in the 1960's and 1970's are still in existence today. The use of the two-digit shortcut for efficiency is still utilized to some extent.

The Y2K problem originated with an attempt to save storage space and money. One way to save space was to abbreviate. Many common abbreviations today did not exist before the computer era. One of those abbreviates had to do with dates.

Thus the year 2000 computer problem or Y2K, dates back to the birth of computers. In the beginning of the computer era dates were stored as only six digits. Thus on January 1, 2000, older computers and older software will see the dates as 01/01/00. The computer will not know if the 00 stands for 1900 or 2000 or for that matter the year 1000.

Since computers and their software use dates to perform many functions such as calculating mortgages or ordering supplies, problems arise.

So, why did programmers use only six digits, why

didn't they do it right to start with?

> *In the late 1960's and early 1970's mainframe computers took up entire rooms or even entire floors of office buildings, yet had very little storage capacity. Shaving off two digits from the dates saved space and money! In 1963 the cost of one megabyte of memory cost thousands of dollars. In the 1970's it cost hundreds of dollars. Today the cost is about one dollar.*

As mentioned above the programmers simply deleted the "19" and instructed the computer to read any digit in the year "field" containing two digits as four digits for the actual display. So a 46 in the year field was read as 1946 and a 77 was read as 1977. The obvious problem again is '00'. Does '00' refer to 1900 or 2000 or 1500?

To save money and space the programmers of the 1960's and 1970's put off the inevitable problem of dealing with the actual century a given date occurred in. The computer was instructed to assume the date occurred in the 20th Century. This six digits issue did not just remain in the area of mainframes. As the industry grew and computer chips were placed in various types of machines the problem was still not addressed.

Many auto manufacturers, for example, have a chip that turns on a light on the dashboard of more expensive cars to tell the owner when to service the car. The chips work on mileage versus time. If the oil has not been changed for three thousand miles and three months have gone by the light comes on. To do this a second chip containing a clock must work at all times.

Inside most computers at least one chip (or CMOS - for complementary metal oxide semiconductor) has BIOS software "burned" into it. On some older computers the BIOS can never be changed. Modern computers, however, have a "flash" BIOS feature than can be updated. When a computer is turned on the BIOS (Basic Input-Output System) burned in the chip gives the computer its initial instructions. The BIOS will check the real-time clock operated by another chip for the time and date. What happens if the BIOS does not understand the date issued by the clock? Will the computer still boot-up? In most cases yes. A fail-safe is added in case the battery running the clock goes dead.

The real-time clock in a computer is always operated with a battery. When the battery goes dead the BIOS cannot obtain a date and none of the time sensitive software will work properly even when the computer boots up. An example would be your dentist's appointment book stored in his computer.

Even if a computer does display a year with all four digits this does not mean the date is stored that way. In the business world this problem became apparent very early. Thirty-year bonds sold in 1970, for example, were to come due in the year 2000. Computers tracking bonds had to be able to work into the year 2000 almost from the beginning of the computer era.

Unfortunately some large organizations such as the Social Security Administration did not have as much foresight as bond salesmen. Because of the huge number of recipients to track, large government agencies such as this made no provision for the year 2000. They needed the 'space' on the old tape drives and all thoughts of the future departed them.

That is one explanation. There may be a second explanation not as complex. One of the main reasons the problem may have arisen is because of the size of a paper 'punch' card.

The first big mainframes could not have hundreds of people typing data into them at once. The data was first 'key punched' on a card. The cards had 80 character columns. All of the information about a record had to fit on that card. For a new Army recruit everything about him had to fit on that one card. His health records, his education—everything. It can be seen why all the information was abbreviated, even the date.

It had to be an issue of space because it was not an issue of technology. An IBM programmer by the name of Robert Bemer developed a cure for the Y2K problem in the 1950's. The Mormon Church wanted one of the new computers to tackle a massive project on genealogy. The software available just would not work because of the date issue. Bemer invented the means to deal with the four-digit issue, even on older computers. He had a forty year lead on the Y2K problem. The technology was there.

But, Bemer's fix was ignored by his bosses at IBM and by most of the industry. At the time, IBM was the industry leader. Had IBM gone to Bemer's four-digit fix and away from the space saving two-digit system we would not have to clean up the Y2K mess today at such a great cost.

The Year 2000 issue is not difficult to understand from the technical point of view. It is the scope of affected systems and business processes that makes this problem so challenging.

Microsoft, the national leader in the design and sale of software, has made this official statement:

"Unfortunately, there will be no simple fix to the year 2000 issue, no 'silver bullet,' due to the fact that the use of dates for calculations is pervasive throughout software and that usage is not standardized. Technically, the problem is simple to understand.

The scope of the problem, however, makes it difficult. Every piece of hardware, software, and embedded system must be taken into account. Everything from mission-critical central accounting systems to small convenience applications must be examined for date-handling and how those dates might affect the rest of the environment." [10]

Bill Gates, the Chairman and CEO of Microsoft Corporation states:

> *"We are committed to providing the information you need to evaluate the impact of the Year 2000 on your computing environment. Microsoft understands that Year 2000 concerns extend beyond technical considerations. The Year 2000 Resource Center addresses the driving business challenges faced by all organizations as they work to remedy this worldwide problem."* [11]

Microsoft's official statement is that all software it currently produces is ready to operate in a year 2000 environment:

"A Year 2000 Compliant product from Microsoft will not produce errors processing date data in connection with the year change from December 31, 1999 to January 1, 2000 when used with accurate date data in accordance with its documentation and the recommendations and exceptions set forth in the Microsoft Year 2000 Product Guide, provided all other products (e.g., other software, firmware and hardware) used with it properly exchange date data with the Microsoft product. A Year 2000 Compliant product from Microsoft will recognize the Year 2000 as a leap year." [12]

We can expect some computer glitches at the turn of the century, but it is not as if that is a problem we don't face every day. One must realize that computer failures happen every single day, even in big companies.

One financial giant, Charles Schwab, has had numerous problems with its online brokerage division. A few lines from a news article sum up the type of problems Schwab has had:

"Charles Schwab's Internet site shut down

for more than an hour Wednesday, proving that even the largest electronic brokers aren't safe from technical glitches.

"Schwab's popular Web site went down at 9:37 a.m. ET, shortly after the stock market opened, typically the busiest time of day for on-line stock trading. Service was restored around 11 a.m. ET.

"During the outage, on-line investors couldn't trade stocks or mutual funds, get stock quotes or use other services on Schwab's Internet site (which accounts for 39 % of all on-line stock trades)." [13]

Computer problems existed twenty years ago, they exist today, and they will exist at the stroke of midnight, December 31, 1999. Computers just don't work right twenty-four hours a day, seven days a week. Problems such as those suffered by Schwab will continue to exist with or without Y2K.

The production of this book, Stop The Y2K Madness, was delayed by several days because of a computer failure. The last week of April 1999 during a server crash large sections of the book were lost. Chapter Five was completely destroyed and had to be re-entered into a separate file and re-edited. Computer failures are common events now and will continue to be well into the next century with or without Y2K.

Many thousands of programmers are working overtime to make sure their companies' computers will continue to operate in the year 2000 and beyond. With new ways of overcoming the computer problems, particularly the Y2K problem, the future digital era does not seem to be impaired.

With optimism we say, "Bring on the New Year." Yet, there are fatalists in America with attitudes that cause many to despair about the coming of the year 2000.

Y2K
Armageddon:

Apocalyptic
Bandwagon of "Hype"

CHAPTER 3

One of the reasons there is so much alarm about Y2K is that many people now feel they cannot believe what they are told by anyone in the government. They do not know whom to trust. This is the natural result of having an admitted liar in the White House. Virtually every department of the current Administration has been investigated for corruption at some level. As a result, government agencies can make numerous pronouncements about how they are ready for Y2K, but many people are not prepared to believe this Administration. Unfortunately, this aids the purveyors of doom in their relentless sales pitch to sell dried food.

However, with some notable exceptions, people in authority do not have a reason to lie about preparations for the Y2K bug. There are those in government who would use Y2K to increase their power over the people. There are those who believe that government should replace both the family and God as the source of authority.

Just as *Stop The Y2K Madness!* was going to press, the authors learned of a special unit formed by Attorney

General Janet Reno. The Unit, called the National Domestic Preparedness Office, was set up for the sole purpose of putting down any civil disorder caused by Y2K panic. The unit is secretly funded by the discretionary funds Janet Reno has available to her in the Justice Department. The principle training is being conducted at the Marine Corps base Quantico and involves the FBI and units of the Marines. Why does this unit exist when the Administration knows that Y2K will be a technological non-event?

Then there are others in government who could benefit from Y2K fears in the public. The Internal Revenue Service, for instance, stands to make a handsome profit from the capital gains tax levied on people who cash out long-held investments or real property in order to buy gold coins and stash them in the basement.

In this Y2K scenario the Internal Revenue Service will be in a state of glee over a capital gains windfall. If people get nervous over the Y2K event and sell off the assets they have held for many years, they will have to pay capital gains on their increase. This would provide our government a huge one-time bonanza. Those that realize too late that their families will go on, even after January 1, 2000, will have lost much to taxation.

Those unfortunate people who follow the advice of the alarmists will cash in stocks and bonds they have held for many years. In some cases up to a full third of their investments will be lost to the IRS. Those professing the end of civilization because of Y2K do not warn people whom they advise what will happen if the IRS is up and running in the year 2000, which it will be.

Having given a warning about certain elements within the government, let us make clear that we the authors do not believe there is a widespread government conspiracy concerning Y2K. We have asked ourselves who else would benefit besides those mentioned above, and who would join this conspiracy?

Surely not the military, most of whose ranks loathe their service under a draft dodger and war protester who has no understanding of military life. The vast army of bureaucrats and appointees will follow Clinton-but only to a point. They don't want a Y2K disaster any more than other Americans do. After all, they all have pension plans and investments, own houses and have children in school just like other Americans.

We believe that the majority of people in the government are taking their responsibilities seriously and are working hard to ensure that their departments will be Y2K compliant.

And so it is with the Congress-they have no desire to see their own lives and careers bite the dust. The Senate Special Committee on the Year 2000 Technology

Problem, made up of both Democrats and Republicans, is charged with investigating what needs to be done to prepare the nation for the millennium change. If they should fail in this assignment and let the nation plunge into chaos without warning, they would be booted out of office in disgrace. They have every motivation to be thorough and truthful in their investigations.

Besides a select group in government who have a "Y2K agenda", there are others who stand to gain from Y2K anxiety. They are the leaders of doomsday cults which have surfaced as the new millennium approaches.

As the year 2000 gets closer, these millennial cults are becoming more and more frenzied. After all, the year 2000 is the last year of the century. To the normal, balanced thinking American, some of these panic promoters act like a conspiracy unto themselves. It is truly unfortunate that many of these groups claim their roots in the Christian church.

Besides those we have mentioned who are seeking power, there are countless others whose motivation for stirring up Y2K dread is financial.

One of the most visible and influential groups with an alarmist Y2K message is the Year 2000 National Education Task Force. This group has captured the attention of the nation, not only for their fatalistic approach to Y2K, but for their moneymaking acumen.

Of that group, probably the most extreme is Michael S. Hyatt, author of the best-selling Y2K book, *The Millennium Bug.* In one statement of pure fantasy he writes, "You could lose electricity—-not just for a couple of hours or days, but for weeks, months, or even years."[14]

The statement that power may be lost for months or even years is just irresponsible. Mr. Hyatt ignores readily available information. The nation's power grid is manually operated, but more on that later.

It would be hard to find a more gloomy report than that found in *The Millennium Bug.* At $24.95 a copy, his book is selling in the hundreds of thousands. There is not a lot of incentive to shut down a moneymaking machine this big, even when the facts point out that his every premise is wrong. Hyatt also offers a special resource manual *Countdown to Chaos* for $89.95. The big question is this: did this $89.95 "manual" cost even $10.00 per copy to produce?

According to Hyatt's books and his statements, much of his argument rests on a perception that is now several years old: "Billions of lines of code must be corrected in millions of computers. Unfortunately, there are not enough programmers, and there isn't enough time." [15]

Mr. Hyatt should research what is happening now in the computer field, not what his projections were several years ago. The reality is that all critical systems in America will have been fixed long before January 1, 2000.

It is ironic that computers and software are being made Y2K compliant very rapidly by some of the same computer experts who initially predicted it would take many years to correct several million lines of code. These computer gurus are also making many millions of dollars fixing the Y2K problem. Unfortunately for them the task is taking far less time than was at first believed. These gurus will make a bunch of money for only a short time. Y2K problems that had been predicted to take years to fix have been done in months and sometimes weeks with the aid of new software.

Hyatt's self-proclaimed positive attitude is not much in evidence when he says, "Preparing for Y2K is like taking out an insurance policy: Hope for the best, but plan for the worst."

In *The Millennium Bug,* Hyatt predicts the worst: ".... we will be living in a 'new dark age' and all that that will mean: war, famine, and pestilence." [16]

Hyatt envisions government agencies failing, hospital emergency room machines stopping, banks closing, social security checks stopping (which will cause anarchy), credit cards being rejected, long-term power failures, military defenses failing, and on and on.

Almost all of his doom and gloom assumptions were made prior to 1998. His predictions were exaggerated even then considering the limited information available at the time. Hyatt is unwilling to update those horrific predictions with honest or new data, because he will have nothing to sell.

Facts change daily, particularly those that have to do with the technology sector. But apparently the draw of the almighty dollar to those in the Y2K doomsayers' circle is too strong to resist now.

Y2KCPR Critical Preparation Resource which sells for $4.95 per issue (there are several issues) includes the following authors: Michael S. Hyatt, Craig Smith, Dr. Ed Yardeni, Ed Yourdon, Senator Robert Bennett, Paloma O'Riley, Karen Anderson, James Stevens, Tim and Teresa Wilson, Tony Keyes, Ken Klein, Rick Cowles, Jim Lord, Ed Bell, Ed Meagher, D.L. Moore and others.

These 'experts' are the core group promoting Y2K fears, although Senator Robert Bennett has recently changed his views and is no longer calling for alarm. Until the others are willing to update their information, statistics and predictions about the future with real data, we must hold them responsible for any Y2K civil unrest, including violence and riots.

Craig Smith is one of the wealthiest Y2K purveyors of panic. He is the author of the much-promoted

Y2KCPR booklet distributed by many major ministries. Smith's appearances with Christian television personalities have helped him sell over one million copies of *Y2KCPR*. His appearances on television have done much to promote panic in the Christian community. However, he does not call it panic. In his words, it is "awareness."

Craig Smith heads the Swiss America gold coin operation, based in Phoenix, Arizona. He is making a lot of money selling gold coins, mostly using a Y2K scare sales pitch.

In the past Smith has been a large contributor to the largest Assembly of God church in the United States. As a result his Y2K gold coin sales pitch is accepted without question by many church members.

To be fair, we should mention that unlike many of the gold coin dealers who are capitalizing on the Y2K panic, (see Chapter five) Smith genuinely believes in financial turbulence to be brought about by Y2K, according to people inside his organization. But, does he realize that much of that turbulence may be caused by his sales techniques?

Dr. Ed Yardeni is the most respected professional within this inner group of Y2K people. He is the chief economist and managing director of Deutche Morgan Grenfell Bank Securities in New York. His dismal prediction of "... a 40 % risk of worldwide recession that will last at least 12 months starting in January, 2000" [17] has been repeated by many worldwide. Despite his expertise, stellar professional background, and his startling testimony before the U.S. Senate Banking Committee (November 1997), which also created panic there, we totally disagree with his statement.

First, most of the world has been in recession for several years. Japan is in its fifth year in a recession that many call a depression. Europe has been in recession since 1997 and Latin America for the past two years. For the most part the recessions have been caused by protectionism and poor central bank management and have nothing to do with Y2K. Only the American economy continues to expand unabated partially because of our superior technology.

In addition, a lot of progress has been made on Y2K issues in financial establishments since his 1997 statement. Dr. Yardeni's statement continues to be used by the doom salesmen even though he has been proven wrong by the rest of the financial world.

Ed Yourdon and his daughter Jennifer wrote the best-selling book, *Time Bomb 2000* ($19.95) They give specific predictions about every aspect of our lives, as to what Y2K would cause. The very title of their book gives an idea of the explosion in society they envision. Yourdon has moved his family from New York City into the country to escape what he believes is an impending disaster.

Senator Robert Bennett is the original "Paul Revere for Y2K" in the federal government. Even his original dismal predictions for the year 2000 have now been tempered with genuine restraint. He is the Chairman of the Senate Special Committee on the Year 2000 Technology problem.

It is unfortunate that Bennett was given the responsibility for the Year 2000 Technology Committee. He has a history of association with Utah survivalist groups. He also sees Y2K from a Mormon perspective. The Mormon Church requires its members to store months' worth of food in preparation for the End Time. He is viewing Y2K from a Mormon perspective, a perspective that requires preparedness for disaster not shared by other denominations.

Paloma O'Riley, co-founder of the Cassandra Project, has one of the most-visited web sites about Y2K. Her web site is quite thorough, especially in her focus on public health, safety and community preparedness. In spite of her 'don't run for the hills' message, her efforts have alarmed many in hundreds of communities across the United States. She encourages a 'Millennial Neighborhood Watch' which is an invasion of everyone's privacy, especially knowing that the Y2K problem is diminishing!

Karen Anderson calls storing large amounts of food "an evangelical device". She claims that telling people that Y2K will bring chaos is a way to lead them to Christ. She expects a devastating economic depression, with many people hungry and standing in bread lines, others looting and killing to get what they want. She says to be prepared for bank runs and long power failures. She continues to teach others to store water and food, while educating women on Y2K. She also runs a booming freeze-dried food business out of the garage of her house in Hurst, Texas. Evangelizing unbelievers by frightening them has never had much of a long-lasting affect.

James Stevens is the author of *Making the Best of Basics* ($24.95) and *Don't Get Caught With Your Pantry Down* ($29.95). Both books have sold well over 500,000 copies. Not bad for a Y2K panic leader whose focus is the food storage business.

Ken Klein is the producer of the mediocre quality video *The Millennium Bug* which he sells for $129.95. Videocassettes are mass-produced for movie producers and large ministries at a cost of between $1.00 and $3.00 depending upon length, quality of tape and jacket production. Not a bad mark-up to $129.95.

Rick Cowles, who has the ear of Pat Robertson, is a sought-after speaker who portrays the year 2000 as a time of disaster. His book, *Electric Utilities and Y2K* sells for $39.95. Cowles never refers to the Edison Institute in his public remarks and for good reason. The Edison Institute has been remarkable in its publishing of up-to-date material on utilities and Y2K. If he referred to the Edison Institute, Cowles would have nothing to sell. Chapter seven of this book has a more complete response to claims about Y2K utility issues.

Jim Lord is the author of *A Survival Guide to the Year 2000 Problem.* ($29.97) He also publishes the *Year 2000 Survival Newsletter* with monthly updates to the book for $129.00 per year. Of course, Lord accepts subscriptions that expire well into the year 2000. He never says how the newsletter will be delivered with the predicted collapse of the Post Office and all computer systems.

Perhaps the loudest of the doomsayer voices is that of Gary North. His Internet site has the most amount of doom and gloom information of just about any in the category. The North site has caused many individuals to buy everything from dried food to bottled water and other products they will never have cause to use in an emergency.

"A disaster looms..." is the cry coming forth from Gary North.

North's much-heralded report on what could happen to the water supply in this country can be categorized as practically "bunk." (See chapter 7).

On his web site, North holds out no hope that disaster can be averted. He says:

> *"I don't mean that society is running out of time to fix this problem. Society has already run out of time for that. There are not enough programmers to fix it. The technical problems cannot be fixed on a system-wide basis. The Millennium Bug will hit in 2000, no matter what those in authority decide to do now. As a system, the world economy is now beyond the point of no return. So, when I say "we," I mean you and I as individuals. We are running out of time as individuals to evade the falling dominoes.*[18]

Thanks to the fear inspired by Gary North and the others selling similar doom books and tapes, a run on the banks and other even worse kinds of chaos could result.

Even political heads of state have added fuel to the fire, like British Prime Minister Tony Blair. Blair, who is often referred to in Washington inner circles as Bill Clinton's finger puppet said, "The Millennium Bug is one of the most serious problems facing not only British business but the global economy today." [19]

Blair, who is a Socialist at heart, has good reason to make such a declaration. He may soon propose sweeping legislation that will allow his left-of-center government to stick their nose into the private British computer industry as well as virtually every British household.

The Gartner Group, Inc. has been working on Y2K since 1980. They claim there are about 25 billion chips in use today and at least 50 million microprocessors have Y2K "anomalies". They also conclude in their materials that, "If only 2% of all programs fail, there will be a total collapse of society, as we know it." The Gartner Group also indicates that "possibly 40 % of all businesses will fail as a direct result of Y2K problems." [20]

This statement is of course illogical at its face value. To claim that a 2% chip failure rate will cause 40% of all businesses in the United States to fail is false, bordering on the ridiculous. Many organizations that have made statements like this in the past have become too embarrassed even to offer retractions.

When will reality set in? Most embedded chips don't even care what date it is. Statements like those of the Gartner Group have given rise to fears that coffee makers and refrigerators will not work on January 1, 2000. Don't worry, your fancy toaster doesn't care what date it is; it only tells the bread to pop up at a pre-set temperature.

A number of individuals and organizations have been

mentioned in this chapter whom the authors do not agree with. The reader is reminded that the authors do not endorse the statements of any of these individuals, their books or their organizations. Those mentioned may very well be responsible for much of the calamity they predict. There is a big difference between alerting and alarming!

4

Exposing the
Prophets *(Profits)*
of Doom
and Gloom

CHAPTER 4

"The End Of The World! Y2K insanity! Apocalypse Now! Will computers melt down? Will society? A guide to Millennium Madness" were the headlines on the front cover of the January 18, 1999 *TIME* magazine. The compilation of stories was a "spoof" aimed at the doomsayers in Christian leadership. The Christ-like figure that appeared on the front cover of the magazine made a mockery of both Christ and evangelical Christians. Without the wild-eyed Y2K fear mongers in the Christian community, the attack on the faith of evangelical Christians would not have been possible.

Profit making "experts" who initially alerted evangelical leaders to Y2K have led many Christian television evangelists and leaders astray. Unfortunately, seeking profit, they held back many vital facts to make the situation look as bad as possible.

Many of the Christian leaders mentioned here are actually good friends of the authors'. Unfortunately, as these friends of ours repeat the Y2K end time scenario, their followers treat that "prophetic" word as a new gospel unto itself.

> *"For God hath not given us the spirit of fear; but of power, and of love, and of a sound mind."*
>
> — *II Timothy 1:7*

God is not the author of confusion. In the above verse, the word "fear" is a spirit. The Word of God is talking about the natural element of fear here, not the awesome fear of the Lord we should have. The "spirit of fear" which is addressed here, prevents a man from operating in faith in the power of God. It is associated with weakness, selfishness, and confusion (the opposites of power, love and a sound mind.)

Some Christian leaders are taking their congregations to a place of fear they should not be led to. These Christian leaders are getting their information about Y2K from those who would make a worldly, not heavenly profit.

> *"For ye have not received the spirit of bondage again to fear; but ye have received the Spirit of adoption, whereby we cry, Abba, Father."*
>
> — *Romans 8:15*

"There is no fear in love; but perfect love casteth out fear: because fear hath torment. He that feareth is not made perfect in love."
— *I John 4:18*

Many Christian leaders have been fed false information by those who prey upon the Christian community for profit. These respected leaders, instead of concentrating on their opportunity to pray, have fallen prey to those, armed with half-truths, who claim the end is in sight. Too often for those selling panic the end they see is the end of the teller line at their bank.

Dr. Jerry Falwell is one of America's foremost Christian leaders. He founded Liberty University, which is perhaps America's premier evangelical Christian institution of higher learning. Dr. Falwell's ministry is very large and includes several publications and TV ministries. He has many assistants and he expects them to do appropriate research before anything appears on his shows or in his publications.

Early on the panic purveyors targeted Dr. Falwell's ministries. They poured books and papers on Dr. Falwell and his assistants giving both him and his assistants and researchers the belief that there was only one side to Y2K.

Using the material passed onto his ministry Dr.

Falwell sounded the Y2K alarm early. In *Y2K: A Christians' Guide to the Millennium Bug,* he writes on page 1:

> *"Would you be prepared to live without electricity for several weeks or even months? No electricity means the bank's computers can't run and your funds will be inaccessible, clean water cannot be pumped into your home, your heat cannot run, your refrigerator and stove and other basic tools will not be in operation."*

> *"Are you prepared to not receive your social security checks, your employer's paycheck, your tax returns, and possibly be without food and household items (such as toilet paper) set aside to last until electricity is restored and your local grocery store is back in operation? These are just some of the examples of the far-reaching implications of Y2K."*

> **"Many reasonable persons are making practical preparations for a possible national crisis.... Begin now to insure your readiness for what may be the worst disaster our world has experienced in cen-**

turies." **(Y2K: A Christian's Guide to the Millennium Bug,** *by Dr. Jerry Falwell*)

Dr. Falwell has backed away from many of his initial remarks, as the truth becomes apparent. Unfortunately, his ministry had already sold thousands of copies of a three-volume video which is still out there spreading misinformation.

The Inspirational Network (former PTL Network) originally aired three Y2K Specials in October and November 1998. Like Dr. Falwell's specials, much of the material was out of date before it aired. That did not stop the network from putting it on the air again, without any crucial updates, in February 1999. While offering their three-tape video series for $29.95, (and other alarmists' books and videos), they tell us, "We are sounding the alarm. There is a coming storm. There can be chaos affecting every family!"

We agree with their prudent advice taken from scripture, "A prudent man sees danger and takes refuge . . . but the simple keep going and suffer for it." (Proverbs 22:3) We only wish they would update their "storm warnings."

INSP's *Family Preparation Guide* gives a 13-month offer of what you and your family should do, month-by-month. This guide prepares a family for months and months of hardship that will allegedly be caused by Y2K.

Many poorer Christian families could be caused financial harm if they followed this plan.

Highlighted in the network video is the CEO of Christian Financial Concepts, Larry Burkett, who has long predicted a coming storm. Burkett, in his newsletter *Money Matters: A Christian Economics Newsletter,* advises people to buy a generator. He goes on to recommend stashing some cash to be ready for the possibility that it may be impossible to get money from the bank. Enough paper money in small denominations and coins to last for one month might prove very helpful, according to his newsletter.

What kind of sound economic advice is it to hide money under your mattress? Burkett is supposed to be one of the "softer" voices concerning Y2K. What he is telling Christians to do is to start a run on the banks! This is not of God; this is very shortsighted, especially for a well-known financial planner.

Although Larry is well respected in the Christian community for financial planning, his investment advice leaves a lot to be desired. No one questions Dr. Burkett's sincerity or honesty; however, after telling people on his nationally syndicated radio show not to invest in the stock market, it has since tripled in value. Those who took $10,000 out of the market on his advice have lost a profit of $20,000 or more. After he advised people to invest in gold, the price collapsed to less than half of what it was when he told Christians to buy!

Larry Burkett, a supposed clear-thinking, conservative, Christian financial leader, actually admitted on national television that he had "stored up months of food, and ski suits to keep warm, just in case." If he purchased this ski clothing because he enjoys skiing then that's great. To buy ski clothing to live in because of a fear of no heat is ridiculous.

People should be informed about Y2K and the potential glitches. But to tell Christians to store up months or years of food, blankets, batteries, and gas and buy generators, under the "disguise" of "preparation guides," is one step from outright misleading the faithful.

Dr. Benjamin Keyes, internationally-known Christian psychologist, explains, "Anytime a spiritual leader stands in front of a group and says, 'We need to be prepared for something,' depending upon where and who it is, their constituents not only take notice, but become concerned about whatever the particular issue is, especially Y2K."

"In the case of the elderly, I think that is particularly true. Not only would they be concerned, but they would take a lot of the messages and preparations to heart. It tends to foster an era of skepticism and panic. Unfortunately, in the area of Y2K, it is panic about

something that is minute."

Back in the late Sixties, we had a mass hysteria around the Second Coming of Christ, which periodically repeats itself. The reality is no one knows the day, nor the time."

"Y2K is over-blown. It is an issue that is being created and generated based upon people's fear. Yes, there are going to be computer glitches, etc. But it is not going to cause the mass problems that some doom-sayers are predicting. Most of the areas have already been corrected." [21]

Christian author David Wilkerson has always painted bleak pictures of what the future will hold and Y2K is no exception for him. In addition to quoting many older "facts" given many months ago, he adds his own twist:

"What do I believe about all of this? (Meaning the doomsday predictions he quotes) I believe it could be that which dramatically helps precipitate the depression I have been warning about.... Years ago I sent out a warning entitled 'Destroyed by a Moth,' based on Isaiah 51:8: 'The moth (which is a bug) shall eat them up like a garment, and the worm (bug) shall eat them like wool.' We have worshiped and idolized our technology—-and how ironic that our nation could be humbled, not by a mighty army, but by a bug—-a worm—-a moth eating away at the cloth of our technology!

Amazing! What an awesome God we serve!" [22]

There is a larger problem with those, like David Wilkerson, who preach Y2K as an End Time event. When this does not come to pass, who will have lied? The Scriptures? Prophecy statements which take Bible verses out of context can only serve to discourage those who are seeking God.

Dr. Grant Jeffrey, a leading speaker on the prophetic and future events, has written a best-selling book, *The Millennium Meltdown.* This is yet another doomsayer book being sold by major Christian publications and pushed by TV ministries. In *The Millennium Meltdown* he states: "This crisis may set the stage for the coming world government that was prophesied to arise in the last days." [23]

December 31, 1999 will probably be a non-event as far as the prophesied End Time or Second Coming of Christ. Y2K very likely has absolutely nothing to do with any specific prophecy or scripture.

Another large ministry that has fallen victim to the Y2K panic purveyors is that of Dr. Pat Robertson. Like Dr. Falwell, Dr. Robertson must rely upon his staff to do the research for what appears in his publications and on his TV show.

Dr. Robertson, founder of the 700 Club and the Christian Broadcasting Network and former presidential candidate in 1988, declared in a late February report that "the United States Military will not be Y2K compliant until the year 2008." Yet, less than two weeks later, those statistics were updated on March 2 to say that "our defense department would be Y2K compliant in time." There were many who knew this report was going to prove Dr. Robertson wrong, but the information never got to him.

Unfortunately, like many Christian broadcast organizations, CBN has not recalled any of the material released and tends to re-broadcast out of date information on Y2K. Several Y2K Television specials that millions have watched were supposed to be "preparing the people". This out of date material is pushing Christians into a panic mode. The CBN website as of May, 1999 still contained outdated material that could cause people to panic over Y2K.

Besides being a Christian leader and author, Dr. Robertson is also a wealthy private businessman. He and his son own ventures all over the world including a diamond mine in Africa. His private ventures have taken the appropriate measures to deal with Y2K, as has his TV network.

Morris Cerullo has a new book entitled, *January 1, 2000: The Day The World Shuts Down.* The title alone tells us how Mr. Cerullo feels about the Y2K problem; no further explanation is necessary. The very title of the book is alarmist. The world will not shut down.

Even some of this nation's more responsible leaders have been hooked by the doom purveyors.

Dr. James Dobson, the most respected Christian psychologist and leading Christian family activist, has highlighted Y2K on his radio programs many times, beginning in October of 1998 with a "distinguished" panel. Unfortunately, on that panel, was Michael Hyatt, a promoter and salesman who is a self-proclaimed Y2K expert. Just being on the Dobson program gave this purveyor of doom respectability.

Along with many others, Dobson believes that if Christians have food stored up for Y2K, we can give it out to those in need, as "a witnessing opportunity for Christ." In other words, if Y2K is a problem let the poor starve, if it is not a problem then we will give them food. Is this what Christ had in mind?

Dr. Jack Van Impe's new video, *2000 Time Bomb* puts fear into the hearts of his viewers with statements such as, "The time bomb is about to go off—-and the enormity of potential disaster awaiting the American people and the world in the year 2000 has been hidden from you and your family!"

And in the same video Dr. Van Impe continues, "See how the effects of this predicted computer catastrophe coincide with Bible prophecy regarding the coming of the Lord and the latter days of time on this earth!"

Christian television's Benny Hinn and James Robinson have both addressed the Y2K "potential crisis problem" by having as their guest Craig Smith. Smith's book, *Y2KCPR,* has sold millions of copies and his gold coin enterprise has made done very well with Y2K.

These Christian leaders are responsible for the millions their programs have affected (or infected).

Those who would cause panic in the church have led even Dr. D. James Kennedy astray. Millions of TV viewers were watching his January 24, 1999 television broadcast centered on Y2K when he quoted from Dan McAlvey, one of the leaders of panic.

Dr. Kennedy stated, "We are in a great race against time. We are racing against the clock, unless Christ returns. All kinds of strange things will happen. I don't know if 25%, 50%, or 75% of what others are predicting will come true. But we should prepare for 75% of that!"

Dr. Tommy Barnett, pastor of Phoenix First Assembly of God, has held Y2K conferences, where even Pat Boone got in on the Y2K scare. Barnett has organized an "Emergency Disaster Task Force" to prepare his people. However, in spite of one of his biggest donors being doomsayer and gold-seller Craig Smith, Barnett has remained balanced in his preaching.

Dr. Tim LaHaye says, "Y2K very well could trigger a financial meltdown, leading to an international depression, which would make it possible for the Anti-Christ or his emissaries to establish a one-world currency or a one-world economic system, which will dominate the world commercially until it is destroyed." [24]

Thousands of churches of all denominations around the country are holding weekly or monthly Y2K preparedness meetings.

One Florida retreat center is holding a "Millennium Watch." Misinformation continues to do damage as it is passed form TV show to radio show to congregation without being updated.

Dr. Hilton Sutton, with his Mission to America headquarters in Texas, a well-respected prophecy teacher, read by millions challenges all of these purveyors of panic. He writes:

> *"Christians are gullible. You are hearing this 'end of the world' from men of God, not from the world, who are confused and frightened. They do not know the Word of God; or they have chosen not to believe it."*

"Or worse than that, they have seen an opportunity to make money out of it. The preachers that are offering you 'survival packages' are like the money changers who were in the Temple; and should be driven out!" [25]

TIME magazine reports, "Apocalyptic fantasies, which have always been freely available in an atomic-age Christian culture, are about to reach another climax. In these final days of the 20th century, religious millennial-ism has once again found a real world problem on which to hang its visions of doom—-the Y2K computer bug."

"It's the uncertainty that some religious millennial-ists are seizing upon, and in the process moving quickly from the plausible to the hyperbolic. In pulpits and on videotapes, on Christian radio stations and Internet web-sites, there are dedicated prophets of doom. They warn of a cascade of Y2K calamities—-massive power black-outs, the failure of hospital, factory and fire equipment, the collapse of banking, food shortages, riots."

"The Y2K alarmists have no concerns about how their post-millennium credibility will stand. The impulse to find signs of the Second Coming and all its attendant disasters is a durable one. It can thrive in the face of con-tinuing disappointments."

"All the same, in the probable event that the world does not come undone next year, academics like Richard Landes, director of Boston University's Center for Millennial Studies, expect that alarmists 'will be totally discredited. Millennialism will fade rapidly.' His group has a theme chosen for the 2002 edition of the International Conference on Millennialism: *'Millennial Disappointment.'* Good title."

"Apocalyptic imaginings are fun, but they're wishful thinking. It's more likely that the world will just churn on as it is." [26]

We agree.....get ready for yet another "black eye" for the evangelical Christian churches in America. Let Godly reason and balance prevail.

Profiteers and Hucksters:

Put Them Out of Business

CHAPTER 5

Y2K is not just a computer problem; it is an indus-try—an industry built on fear and greed. It has proved to be a real cash cow for a host of writers and entrepreneurs.

One of the most prolific and successful writers about the Y2K issue has been Gary North. He is a Reconstructionist with a fatalistic vision of the future. His organization, Institute for Christian Economics, started selling Y2K preparedness a long time before any-one else. His extensive website presents his view of a catastrophic future. "In all of man's history," he warns, "we have never been able to predict with such accuracy a worldwide disaster of this magnitude. The millennium clock keeps ticking. There is nothing we can do."

"But he has a few recommendations anyhow," notes a recent *TIME* magazine article,"...buy gold and grain; quit your job; and find a remote cabin safe from the riot-ing hordes. He also recommends a two-year subscription (price: $225) to his newsletter, *REMNANT REVIEW,* an offer that appears to reflect a faith that, if nothing else, the mail will keep operating through 2000. As a subscriber incentive he promises 'my report on 15 stocks which stand to benefit from this crisis.'"

TIME Magazine in its January 18, 1999 issue on page 68 had this to say about Gary North and his ability to generate sales: "'Scary Gary's' website is by far one of the most popular Y2K panic centers."

Numerous Y2K pyramid schemes and enterprises appear in many publications and on radio and TV. For example, an advertisement in the "Business Opportunities" section of *USA Today* in January, 1999 sums it all up:

> *Y2K GOLD MINE*
> *Get RICH in GOLD, SILVER and CASH*
> *Call 888-XXX-XXXX (24hrs) ASAP!*

This ad and several others like it promised the same huge profits as those promoting leases of adult web sites and MLM diet fads on the same page. In other words the Y2K ad appeared along with all the other get-rich-quick scams advertised in *USA Today.*

Some operators of Y2K companies will train others (for a price) to sell silver and gold coins to worried people at exorbitant prices. Other companies will teach individuals how to scare families into thinking they will stave to death in the year 2000 unless they purchase thousands of dollars' worth of tasteless and ultimately useless dried food stocks to bury in their back yard. Still other companies will show how to make big bucks selling books, audio and video tapes designed to alarm the public with half truths and out-and-out lies about the Year 2000 computer situation.

Several of these money-making offers will be investigated by the Y2K Information Project of RFC. The primary question is motive. Do the operators of the companies genuinely believe that our society will be rocked to its foundations beginning at midnight on December 31, 1999—or are they selling products they themselves will not buy? One fact points to a common lack of belief in a real computer problem in the year 2000 by those selling Y2K panic materials. Virtually every one of these concerns takes orders using computers. Virtually every one of the companies selling silver and gold accepts plastic to pay for it. They maintain credit card machines and bank accounts because they know what they are selling is a lie, a lie designed to make a profit from fear.

It would seem that the operators of these companies would ask for certified checks or money orders to cash if they feared Y2K as much as they claim. (One organization does ask for several small money orders to be sent, with the payee line left blank. This is presumably to distribute the funds on the pyramid line in such a manner as not to allow the funds to be tracked by the IRS.) In reality they have no need to fear accepting credit cards in payment for their products. In 1995 banks and other institutions sent test credit cards to every store that owned a credit card machine. The merchants were required to run these on their credit card machines to make sure they were Y2K compliant. Those merchants whose machines could not properly pick up dates past 1999 were required to purchase or lease new credit card readers. Since 1997 credit card companies have been issuing cards which expire in the year 2000 and beyond. The fear merchants are more that willing to accept credit cards for payment of their goods even when those cards expire well into the next millennium.

Neither do those selling Y2K have a problem using computers or firms whose business is based on computers. Many of those selling silver and gold, for example, use professional telemarketing companies to take orders for their materials. The person taking a call to sell silver and gold because of the Y2K "end time" may have just finished taking an order for a set of year 2000 encyclopedias.

There are several "key" Y2K dates used to scare the public. One of those falls on September 9, 1999. Computers read the date as 9999. The number 9999 is also the "stop program" code of a computer language known as COBOL. Many companies such as those advertising in *USA Today* cite it as the date the problems really begin. So, do they plan on shutting down prior to this date? Of course not. In reality there are virtually no computers in America that still run on COBOL. This is an old mainframe program written for the Navy. The language is for all intent and purpose dead. The companies selling Y2K survival goods will ignore the date in their own operations because they know their computers will treat September 9, 1999 as just another day for them to rip off fearful people.

Of particular shame are some of the "Christian survivalist" companies that sell gold coins. Not willing to make the standard $15 or $20, a coin profit they are convincing the anxious and unsuspecting to purchase gold and silver coins with "intrinsic" value. That means the coin has extra value because it is rare. As of the writing of this article, gold trades at $295 per once. A one-ounce gold coin should sell for about $315. But some of these operators are selling gold coins from the 1890s that have a "greater" value. An 1890's era one-ounce gold coin in good condition could trade at three of four times its weight value, depending on the date, the mint mark, or other factors that make it a rare find.

If all the Y2K claims are true, then purchasing a one-ounce gold coin for $1,000 is crazy. In a real emergency no one is going to trade food or fuel for a gold coin at an exchange rate three to four times the going price of gold. No one is going to trade $1,000 worth of food for one ounce of gold. How would the farmer or storekeeper one is bartering with know the "intrinsic" value? Only an experienced rare coin dealer or collector would know that, and it can take quite a lot of time and persistence to find someone willing to pay the asking price. In fact, it may be impossible to get the asking price if the coin was bought at too high a price to begin with. Buying gold for panic or war-time situations is best done by weight only. If one can afford it, it is probably a good idea to own a few gold or silver coins in case of an emergency of any kind, not just Y2K. But any huckster who claims a silver or gold coin with "intrinsic" value is a better value during wars, panic or famine is just an outright liar.

A spokesman for a well-known gold and silver trader in Dallas stated that they would make no effort at all to sell ancient gold coins during the Y2K scare. This company, like other reputable coin dealers, offers gold coins at the daily trading rate plus a small handling surcharge. Other reputable coin dealers contacted said they anticipate being offered coins at discounts in the year 2000 as people realize how foolish they were to move major amounts of savings into gold and silver coins.

Warning! It looks as if many people have already sold assets they have held for many years in order to put the proceeds into gold and silver coins. Before anyone does this, they should take a look at what it will mean in taxes. It may mean they will have to pay a large capital gains tax-up to a third of their total investment—to the IRS. And yes, unfortunately the IRS will still be around and functioning in the year 2000.

The advertisements in *USA Today* and other publications for many of these Y2K operators appeared under "Business Opportunities". The promoters' greed has extended to recruiting full time salesmen in major newspaper. Barnum said, "There is a sucker born every minute." Those selling Y2K panic are followers of the Barnum philosophy. Let the buyer beware!

In the 1980's a gentleman donated his collection of Morgan dollars to our ministry on the condition that we offer them at retail prices to ministry supporters to raise funds for evangelism. We have faithfully continued to do just that. We have no problem offering the coins at a retail level because we are not coin dealers. We consider the coins to be in the same class as books and tapes the ministry offers. People are giving a donation to our work, and the books, tapes and coins sent to them are tokens of our appreciation for their financial gift to us. It is our hope, our prayer, that no one believes they will make a profit off of any book, tape, coin or Christmas ornament we send to them as a result of their gift to the ministry.

We never claim that the coins, books or tapes the ministry sends to people will ever make them rich or save their lives or fortunes.

Unfortunately, some ministries related to Y2K industries are just flat lying to people and cheating them. They sell Morgan dollars at up to $50.00 each that are just junk silver. Far from uncirculated, the dates can hardly be read. Coin dealers put these in the category of "junk" silver and the value is perhaps only a few cents above the prevailing spot market for silver, about $5.50 per ounce.

People should easily see through some of the value claims by carefully reading the literature. One company, The Vault, Inc. sells several "Y2K coin sets for $295. One "set" is a single quarter-ounce French Rooster worth perhaps $100. On their multi-level marketing scheme they claim a salesman can make a commission of $1,000 on every 16 sales. But there is more. Their material goes on to claim a 20% bonus on the first down line and a 40% bonus on the second down line. Once all the commissions and bonuses are stripped away, none of the coin sets can have a value of more than about $150 at most and that is before taking out their company's profit.

How can this be a Y2K survival investment when the final purchaser of the coins pays twice the original price?

This same company offers several $295 packets. One of these is a quarter-ounce British Sovereign or a quarter-ounce French Rooster as mentioned above. The company advertises that all gold coins they sell are "pre-1933 with numismatic value." Why buy old coins? They claim the U.S. government cannot confiscate pre-1933 gold coins and this makes them more of a reliable investment than modern coins.

The reality: in a state of martial law the government can confiscate anything including your house and your dog! There is nothing the government cannot confiscate in an emergency at the point of a gun. But the fallacy here is even worse—the idea that in an emergency, such as a famine, that ancient gold coins will have an "intrinsic" value above their actual gold content. The exact reverse is true! In times of famine and war any gold trading will be done with a scale. No one selling food is going to hand out $1,000 worth of food for one ounce of gold because the coin is "collectible". What good is a "collectible" when people are starving? None at all!

The Vault promises a $5,000 per week "potential" for multi-level salesmen plus a 20% bonus for every four sales representatives they recruit, plus a 40% bonus if ten sales representatives are recruited! Their sales material claims another $2,000 to $4,000 off those "down-line" sales. In all, the company claims a potential of about $9,000 per week with little or no effort.

So it is no surprise that the one-quarter-ounce

French Gold Rooster can be purchased wholesale for around $100.

The Vault has other "sets" to offer for $295. One contains six Morgan Silver Dollars. If these are uncirculated (which the company does not claim), they would have a retail value of about $120 to $180 and a wholesale value of about $80 to $100. They bought these coins wholesale and are offering them for about twice retail. They also offer a set of modern American Eagles currently sold by the U.S. government for about ten bucks each. The price at The Vault— thirteen for $295, or $23 each. No wonder they claim multi-level salesmen can make a fortune. All the salesmen have to do is be less than truthful about the value of the coins!

The Vault requires that all sales must be made by money order or cashier's check. There is no place in the company's literature stating a refund policy. There is also no statement or declaration of the real value of the coins sold.

Anyone who wants to get involved in multi-level marketing would probably be well advised to stick to diet fads and vitamins. You can use the vitamins if you can't sell them— you can't eat over-priced silver and gold coins.

A lot of the Y2K multi-level marketing companies really aren't selling anything except information (and highly dubious information at that). One of the most ingenious is Y2K International's "Prepare and Prosper" Pack. The "Pack" contains no gold or silver and no dried food and it costs only $249. For the $249 you receive a "resource guide" a "license" to make five copies of it, a six-video set and twelve audio tapes. The audio and videotapes tell you how to store food, barter items and grow food in a garden. You can also buy the kits wholesale for $200 and make $49 for each one you sell. This is also a multi-level marketing company as are most of the Y2K sales organizations. Beside the $49.00 commission on a sale, a representative can earn $20 per sale override on representatives he recruits. The sales literature shows a potential of $312, 500 or more but does not state in what time frame.

Get this: part of the package is weekly E-mail updates! This from a company that claims virtually every computer in America is going to fail.

How Y2K International wants to be paid is even more curious. Because of the payment system, just about everyone associated with them will be open to an IRS audit. The following instructions were enclosed with their order form:

1) *Fax a copy of the filled out application to*
   888-XXX-XXXX

2) *Go to the nearest Post Office and*

purchase:

   a) 3 postal money orders in the amount
   of $20.00. Leave them blank.

   b) 2 postal money orders in the amount
   of $40.00. Leave them blank.

   c) 1 postal money order in the amount
   of $80.00. Leave it blank.

3) *Fill out a check in the amount of $28.00*
    payable to XXXXXX

4) *Send entire package by Express Mail or*
    overnight carrier to XXXXXXXXXXXXX

Oddly the total does not come to either $200 or $249 but rather to $248. Nothing in the literature explains why, nor is it explained why the new recruit is to send blank money orders. Will the IRS have an interest in where all these blank money orders are going and who is cashing them? You bet!

The hypocrisy of Y2K International is typical of all the outfits selling Y2K doom packets. On one of their lead sales pages they claim that banks will not be Y2K compliant. One bold face screaming text says, "Think Banking, Think Telecommunications. Think Electrical Power. Think Transportation. None of these industries are compliant today." Another boxed item says, "The Year 2000 may be the worst man-made disaster in history"

With all this screaming you would expect the company not to trust banks at all. However, you can fax them your bank account number and they will be happy to auto-draw from your account the $25.00 fee for their monthly "Y2K International" newsletter that can be sent to you by e-mail, fax or regular mail.

On the one hand they claim the banking industry will collapse. On the other hand they want to auto-draw from your bank account using a computer. Then they will e-mail or fax you a monthly newsletter over a telecommunications system that they claim will not work. Either they trust the telecommunications industry to deliver the newsletter for them monthly or they are taking money for a product they don't believe they can deliver. Which is it?

The company will not accept computer error as an excuse if one of these drafts does not clear. They will draft your account a $25.00 fee if the draft bounces. If it bounces a second time they say they demand that you pay, "three times the face value of the check", and they are very blunt is saying they will seek attorney's fees if you don't pay up. Does this mean they believe court computers are going to work?

Many of the Y2K merchants, including Y2K International, seem to spend more time talking about money than the claimed impending disaster. A cover letter sent out by one Y2K salesman is very blunt: "There is no other networking company around that pays this much so quickly," he writes. "But we must make money quickly - can't wait months or years. We need money NOW if we hope to get prepared for what we expect in our particular circumstances from the Y2K event."

The "preparedness kit" that is sold by Y2K International includes instructions in "bartering." It tells the purchaser what items to have on hand to barter for food, etc. because money will have no value in a computerless society. This is yet one more example of playing both sides. If money is not going to be any good, and Americans will have to barter for food, what good is all this money going to do for individuals who participate?

Let's summarize this fine example of one of many Y2K doom purveyors.

They claim telecommunications will not work, but sell a monthly newsletter distributed by e-mail and fax. They claim the banking industry will collapse but ask you to trust them with your bank account number for auto drafts. They say that only bartering will work when civilization collapses, but they claim you can make loads of money following their networking concept. They claim the legal system will collapse but threaten those who give them bad checks with lawsuits and legal fees if checks bounce. This is hypocrisy on a grand scale.

The claims of dried food companies are some of the

most interesting. One company actually advertised that you should order your supply now because there is a backlog of several years in orders, but that they would ship at once.

"There are already small signs of alarm. Preparedness Resources, Inc. is a 20-year-old Utah purveyor of dehydrated foods. The typical order of one year's 'nutritionally balanced' supply of grains, vegetables, fruit, milk, meat substitutes and cooking aids sells for $1,495 plus shipping. Until about 1995, the company did most of its business with Mormons, who stockpile food as a principle of their faith. More recently, however, as much as 90% of sales have been to non-Mormons. 'Y2K is driving the worry,' says office manager Roslyn Niebuhr. Because monthly sales have zoomed from $300,000 in December 1977 to $4 million last November, the company has quadrupled its dealerships to 100." [27]

At Emergency Foods of Lehi, Utah, much of the sales pitch consists of attacks on the competition. Their lead sales letter says, "Dehydrated food supplies diminish daily due to the Y2K crisis. Most food suppliers are currently backlogged 10 to 12 months. Our supplies and prompt delivery are limited. Don't Wait! Getting an emergency supply of food is as important today as boarding the ark was in the days of Noah."

Not satisfied with getting you to buy their product

because of the Y2K issue, they throw in every crisis they can think of. Their advertisement states, "Every day the year 2000 moves closer. This crisis, drastic weather changes, political unrest, and dramatic market changes are responsible for national and word wide shortages." They conclude, " Invest in your food insurance today."

Another of Emergency Foods' sales letters starts off with the headline, Consumer Beware". Under a headline that says "Beware of Wolves in Sheep's Clothing" the company says, "It has come to our attention that several food storage companies continue to take orders they cannot fill. Many of these companies are backlogged 1–12 months. As the urgency in the world situations increase and Y2K looms closer the demand for food storage rises daily." They say that their competitors often "...sell their packages for "50% off, leaving their customers with 50% less food per unit." They conclude that, "It is impossible to resolve problems with a company – who sold improperly packaged food at cheap discounted prices – when they are no longer in business."

After attacking the competition, Emergency Foods goes on to claim that their food has a storage life of twelve years. If we are dealing with the collapse of civilization on January 1, 2000 do we have to be concerned about a twelve-year shelf life of food?

To get customers to buy the food they claim that disaster is at hand. Then they tell you the food will last twelve years. How is this company going to survive 2K? Will they take the food back if there is no Y2K meltdown of society? Again, there are no guarantees from this firm other than to claim that the food will last on your shelf for more than a decade (it will take longer than that to persuade your average kids to eat this stuff).

Emergency Foods sells food packaged by another company, Perma Pak. Their basic food program supplies one adult with 1700 calories a day for one year. The cost (not including wheat or sugar to make bread) is $1,295.00. This is a sizeable investment for many people, and especially so if they have several family members.

Some of the Y2K companies sell everything from windmills to do-it-yourself home burial vaults. If some-one dies after the Y2K "event" it is presumed that under-takers will not be able to embalm them without comput-ers. How embalming has been done for the last 6,000 years without computers no one can explain.

The water issue and the purchase of water barrels are intriguing. The assumption is that cities and counties will not be able to deliver water to homes after January 1, 2000. However, the force of gravity has delivered water for thousands of years. The Romans were probably the best in ancient times at water delivery. Some of the sys-tems they built in Europe were still in operation well into the 20th century. Water is still delivered the same way today. Many water systems do not even have pumps unless the system includes water towers. The water gets to the top of the tower using float-activated pumps much like those in a toilet. When the water level in the tower goes down to a certain point, the float turns on the pump. When the water level reaches a predetermined high point, the float turns the pump off. The water is delivered from the tower to homes and businesses by gravity. Gravity is not run by computers and will be the same on January 1, 2000 as it was on December 31, 1999.

Even though most water tower pumps are controlled by floats or other such devices, there are those who believe there will be no power whatsoever to run the pumps. Our research on power supplies (see Chapter Seven) indicates otherwise. In fact, 97% of all power companies will be Y2K compliant by September of 1999.

Most of the Y2K products, from dried beans to gold coins, are over-priced, and much of it is of low quality. Products such as magnetic chairs to replace the need for doctors is just plain foolish. Before buying anything specifically for the Y2K event, one should think twice. Individuals should ask themselves these questions before buying anything:

Would I buy a year's supply of food for a

hurricane storm warning?

Would I buy a water tank or drill a well for a tornado?

Would I buy an electric generator for a bad snowstorm?

Would I buy gold coins at four or five times their value for a long-term investment?

Some of the answers to these questions may be yes. Someone who lives in a rural area and has had power problems before in snowstorms, should perhaps buy a generator. Perhaps some investment in coins is wise for those who know and understand this type of investment. But someone who has before only invested in stocks and bonds and knows nothing about coins should beware! Investing in coins with "intrinsic" value can be as risky as buying junk bonds.

Pain and Death Caused by Misperceptions, NOT Computers

CHAPTER 6

Pain and death may result from the fear and panic, not from the actual computer problem. Misperceptions and misinformation may very well cause social unrest. One of the main purposes of this book is to help plead with these Y2K anxiety "experts" to change, or at least update their outlandish statements which push people over the edge and influence them to make strange and costly mistakes.

Paul Somerson in an editorial in *PC Computing* magazine (February 1999) vents his frustrations at the Y2K alarmists. His is a purely secular, not a Christian perspective, and he has considerable technical background and experience. In Somerson's article, entitled "HOAX" he describes how "religious zealots" are buying land and moving to remote sites such as High 54 Ranch in Arizona, Prayer Lake in Arkansas, and God's Wilderness in Minnesota. All these new communities began in response to Y2K worries, and new members are asked to bring their own food and ammo.

Somerson asks, "So, is the sky really falling? Will

1/1/00 truly be the Day the Earth Stood Still? Should you buy K rations, and pack heat? Get real." [28] He believes the widespread misinformation comes from two main sources. First, there are the computer system consultants, who are charging hefty sums to get companies ready for the Year 2000. Scare mongering on their part helps to drum up business, and business is very good. Some of these consultants are charging large companies over $100,000.00 per day to make sure they are Y2K compliant.

In addition, Somerson (and he is not alone) says unfounded fear is being promoted by "religious kooks bracing for Armageddon." [29] We are concerned that a lot of unbelievers will see Christians as "kooks" if too many head for the wilderness or get too worked-up over Y2K, which will in all probability not amount to much. This will not make the job of witnessing to the lost any easier-it will only make it harder.

We agree with Somerson when he says that businesses will in their own self-interest, fix the problem in time. He says that businesses aren't stupid; the stock market and most big banks have already addressed the problem.

So have the power companies, according to the North American Electric Reliability Council. They are all so terrified by endless litigation that they will make sure they are ready to handle the dreaded 00.

Many other computer experts and informed people also minimize the problems Y2K will cause. Federal Reserve Board Chairman, Alan Greeenspan got a bad case of the Y2K jitters last year. But he admitted on Friday, February 26, 1999, that "Y2K was an over-kill."

As Fred Moody of ABC News notes on ABC.com, "When it comes to the fizzle factor—-the degree to which an expected event fails to live up to its hype—-the 'millennium bug' (aka Y2K) will prove to be the standard against which all other overhype is measured. Not for 1,000 years or so has so much dread been provoked, and so much money made, in preparation for something that will amount to so little." [30]

Moody goes on to add, "The thing that has always bothered me about the various Y2K doomsday scenarios—-ranging from massive nationwide power failures to the collapse of world financial markets and, eventually, worldwide famine and widespread death—-is that it has always been too perfect a bug for our times. It is too apt a symbol to be real, too ingenious and appropriate an end to 20th century civilization to be credible. The notion that the world will end because of a careless bit of programming of computing machine—-machines, moreover, that have become the 20th century's false gods—-is something that belongs in the realm of fiction or art rather than reality or science." [31]

Unfortunately, through this misinformation and misperception about Y2K, people's lives will be turned upside down. Again, not because of the computer glitch, but because of the hype.

One of the most respected computer experts in the business is Wayne Rash, the Managing Editor of Technology for *InternetWeek* magazine. He says that even computer magazine editors have problems separating what's real from what's hype about year 2000 issues.

He explains, "The problem is made worse because there are any number of people who are intentionally making it so. As bad as the Y2K dilemma is, there is a plethora of consultants and others who profit from frightening potential clients."

"This adds to the hysteria and cuts down on the flow of accurate information, " says Rash. "While it is true that the Y2K problem is finally getting national attention (when was the last time you heard a potential computer problem mentioned in the State of the Union address?), it's surprising how little useful information there is in the public domain. It's almost as if someone were making sure we were kept in the dark." [32]

We like Mr. Rash's suggestion that in order to differentiate between hype and truth, we should all "apply a test of rationality." The first thing he suggests is to ignore the extremes at either end of the question. Those who say we will have no problems at all with Y2K are probably wrong. But so are the ones who predict a great catastrophe. Secondly, Rash suggest we apply "a test for self-interest." We should ask ourselves, "What does this person have to gain by spreading this information? Does he stand to gain financially by selling coins, dried food, generators, newsletters or whatever? If the person does stand to gain financially, then we should at least get a second opinion before buying whatever he is selling.

"Solving the Y2K problem without bankrupting your company is hard enough without interference by people providing bogus or self-serving information. The recommendation I've been giving to those who e-mail me is not to panic. Look for advice in places where the greatest interest is in providing accurate information." [33]

The statements from the real experts, those working on the problems rather than just trying to profit from words, are very different from those of Gary North and company.

Many in the media are getting tired of the hype. Former BBC award-winning journalist Dan T. Wooding suggests, "There is so much nonsense being spread about Y2K. Also, there's a lot of people inciting the fear so they can make money." [34]

Good old American ingenuity is hard at work!

On one hand, the doom and gloom, end-of-the-world pitchmen are hard at work!

At the same time, the computer gurus are getting rich through their efforts to solve the Y2K problem in plenty of time.

When faced with the fact that 99% of critical industries will be Y2K compliant, the doomsayers then call upon the "domino effect." They maintain that since computers communicate with each other, if some computers go down because of a Y2K "bug" it will cause a general collapse of the whole system.

The "domino" effect just does not exist when it comes to computers "talking" to each other. One of the Y2K myths is that if one computer goes down, they all go down because they are connected. Thus, if a small utility company in rural Utah has a power outage because of a computer failure the entire national power grid fails. Not so.

In February of 1999, lightning struck a utility center in Virginia, near our headquarters. The power was knocked out along with all of our computers at our ministry headquarters' office. Our server in Colorado used for our Internet site was not affected when our computers went down here, nor did the lights go out in New York City because there was a failure in Fredericksburg, Virginia.

Most large computers communicate on a peer to peer basis. Peer to peer means that the computers function on their own except to obtain data from each other. The entire Internet is largely peer to peer. If the Religious Freedom Coalition server fails, the Internet does not go down. When someone uses their computer to read information they get a message that says, "Unable to open site" or something like that, depending on the browser they use. Many organizations take their Internet sites down at night for changes and updates. This does not bring the entire Internet down.

The Religious Freedom Coalition has an office network of about ten computers for data processing, payroll, etc. Our computers operate on a peer to peer system. Last December, the computer we use mainly as a server, crashed. When we brought it back on line, a warning came on the monitor that the hard disk had physical damage. We immediately moved all critical data to the computer in bookkeeping over the peer to peer network.

All other computers in the office were then pointed to the "new" server. Indeed the hard disk was bad. It was replaced with two new disks, one for data and one for programs. Once the repair was made all critical data was transferred back to the "old" server.

It is true that many large companies do not have network systems like ours-they have server-based systems.

In these cases all workstations do fail when the server fails. Most companies that use server-based systems are large and also have backup systems. American Airlines has a complete duplicate system for reservations and maintenance that can be brought on line in an instant. Many large corporations have such "mirror" systems. Airlines are another good example of the foolishness of the "domino" theory.

If American Airlines' Sabre reservations system fails, this does not cause the Delta or United Airlines systems to fail. Granted, Delta and United cannot book on American while that system is down, but this does not cause their systems to fail.

There have been widespread predictions the airline reservation systems would fail in early 1999, when year-in-advance reservations would fall in 2000. These predictions have proven false as reservation systems have taken on hundreds of thousands of reservations for the year 2000.

For the purveyors of doom this is bad news. Again, their main theory is based on the assumption that, "If one Chevy truck has a flat and is undrivable, then all Chevy trucks are undrivable." This logic is just as faulty with computers as it is with trucks.

Incidentally, we tested our computers for Y2K. We reset the date for January 1, 2000. All of our programs, even the old DOS payroll program, worked just fine.

Every day, knowledge is increasing by fathom leaps. Even in the short time since many of the "doom and gloom" leaders made their statements (even at the end of 1998), computer knowledge has increased greatly. Y2K plans have had to be changed, simply because of the time factor being lessened considerably, due to new, innovative technology and knowledge. The Bible prophecies of that:

> *"But thou, O Daniel, shut up the words, and seal the book, even to the time of the end: many shall run to and fro, and knowledge shall be increased."*
>
> — *Daniel 12:4*

What about the appliances and services we use every day? Some people are claiming that such devices as pacemakers, streetlights, elevators and cars will not work after midnight on January 1st, 2,000 because they depend to some degree on computers.

Computer experts have precise answers that we can use. One of the very best balanced websites is www.icta.net/y2k. This is the website of Pete Holzmann, who is the Global Coordinator of the AD2000 & Beyond Movement Interactive (Technology) Task Force and President of the International Christian Technologists'

Association (ICTA). Drawing on close to three decades of high tech experience, Holzmann's technical background ranges from mainframe computers to PC's and "embedded systems." He seeks to separate hype from reality.

According to Holzmann, "Pacemakers, street lights, elevators and cars do not care what year it is! Few people actually know the real Y2K facts." Otis Elevator, the largest elevator vendor, has tested all systems and they are confident elevators will function! [35]

He has similar advice for those who claim that televisions, VCR's, microwave ovens, bread makers, even hair dryers will shut down on 1/1/2000. He states, "There is no evidence for any of these scenarios. It is true that dates may be wrong in appliances that track the date (such as VCR's), but no expert suggests the equipment will fail to work!

"Some claim a computer-controlled system cannot survive unless it is 100 percent Y2K compatible. In reality, only critical defects need to be repaired for service to continue. For example, true critical Y2K defects in electric power delivery systems are extremely rare, i.e. things that would cause a serious interruption in power delivery; on the other hand, there are many non-critical Y2K power problems involving accounting reports, etc....

"...It is important to remember that in the real world,

complex systems, whether aircraft or power grids, usually function correctly even when several of their parts are broken. That's how they are designed, and that is how they operate!"

Holzmann continues, "Doomsayers suggest we need to 'head for the hills,' buy weeks or months worth of food, obtain backup power generators, and generally prepare for the reduction of our social services to the level of developing nations.

"Sadly, much of this hysteria comes from within the Christian community. Motivations of such people must be questioned. Some of the best-known spokesmen have a hidden theological agenda, believing the world as we know it must end in the next few years. Also, many doomsayers make a tidy profit from sales of their books and seminars." [36]

There is sound advice from Steve Hewitt, founder and editor-in-chief of *Christian Computing* magazine, who declares, "Some Christians are in full panic. Many others are on the verge. Christians are selling their homes, liquidating their assets and purchasing guns. Is the panic justified? No. Y2K will cause us little more than a bump in the road." [37]

On the Dr. James Dobson radio show panel, Mr. Hewitt was very specific as to the cause of media misinformation: "Christian leaders... present their (Y2K) case using many facts and figures that are either out of date or not properly researched." [38]

There are many who offer calm and hopeful counsel, and who calmly examine the facts. In October 1998, bishops of the Evangelical Lutheran Church in America issued a pastoral letter to their five million members, dismissing "wild prophecies" and declaring that the third Christian millennium should be welcomed with hope! [39]

The Bible has an even more profound view. The Bible has encouraging words for us in uncertain times.

> *"The steps of a good man are ordered by the Lord; and he delighteth in his way.*
>
> *"Though he fall, he shall not be utterly cast down: for the Lord upholdeth him with his hand.*
>
> *"I have been young, and now am old; yet have I not seen the righteous forsaken, nor his seed begging bread.*
>
> *"He is ever merciful, and lendeth; and his seed is blessed." Psalm 37:23-26*

As fear begins to grip many in our nation, we all need to realize that it will not be the end of the world as we know it, as some have suggested. Few people know the facts. More experts need to speak out, experts who are balanced, as opposed to hidden-agenda authors and dried food salesmen who tell us to "head for the hills."

Fear is not of God. Faith is of God.

The Y2K
Problem is Being
Overcome!

CHAPTER 7

As in many of life's situations, those who make rash and hasty decisions based on insufficient information stand to lose a lot of money. Those who manage to stay levelheaded have a good chance to come out ahead. Staying calm during the Y2K event will prevent any great loss of personal wealth. In fact, resisting the urge to panic may result in great wealth as it did for John D. Rockefeller who, during the 1929 stock market crash, used every dime he had to buy stocks. His wealth increased many times because he bought rather than sold.

Y2K compliance changes every single hour. Companies are rushing to insure their profits as we move into the year 2000. In short, the Y2K problem is being overcome!

All truth is based solely upon facts, not human perceptions. Being fearful is more often a perception than a reality. Many people are fearful when they first get into a roller coaster at an amusement park. Is that fear justified given the degree of engineering and maintenance to the ride? No. No one is afraid the ride will come off the rails, rather the fear is a perception of danger. Y2K is much like the fear of getting on a roller coaster.

There is great reason for optimism when we look at how the Y2K problem is being overcome, as there are daily reports surfacing from every area of the economy. Reports at hand from corporations are for the first quarter of 1999 only. This leaves nine months for companies to become Y2K compliant. Every hour, fortunately, the information in this book is superseded by even newer compliant information (to which the alarmists pay little or no attention.)

Of course there is genuine concern for many different aspects of our lives: electric power, national defense, social security, food distribution, banks and currency, credit cards, insurance, investments, oil and gas, communications, airline travel, medical assistance and devices

Let's examine each of the essential major industries.

ELECTRIC POWER

This is a huge concern, because if we do not have power, we lose heat, lights, refrigeration, mass communications such as television, computers, and most of the "comforts" of life.

Will the Y2K millennium bug cause a nationwide blackout on January 1, 2000?

Power loss is a widespread fear, but America's electrical utilities say this fear is groundless. An industry report released in April 1999 paints a positive picture of efforts to correct Y2K software problems and says that if there are any Y2K power outages, they will be local and manageable.

"We didn't find very many problems,' says Gene Gorzelnik, communications director of the North American Electric Reliability Council (NERC). "'The ones we turned up are surmountable. The Y2K problem can be dealt with." [40]

Senator Robert Bennett who is head of the Senate's Y2K Task Force, has been critical of the progress of utility companies in the past. Early this year, though, he reduced his "blackout prediction" from 40% to 4%. And more recently his predictions of disaster have been scaled back even more.

"Experts fully expect power delivery in the USA to continue on 1/1/2000, with possible short-term interruptions in localized rural areas," according to an ABC News investigative report by Chris Stamper. He found that "Critical power delivery systems worldwide generally do not depend on dates." [41]

Why is there such a sudden confidence?

According to David Swanson, Vice President of Environmental Affairs at the Edison Electric Institute,

"The U.S. electric supply and delivery systems are not heavily reliant on computers and electronic controls. Those operations that do rely on computer systems can be manually operated in emergencies - and often are during power outages arising from storms or mechanical problems. We are accustomed to dealing with unplanned events. While Y2K is a unique occurrence, it is a planned event." [42]

Virtually all electric utility companies have been seriously developing their plans of what to do in case of problems caused by Y2K. Practically all employees will be on call for duty during December 31, 1999 and January 1, 2000. Fortunately, the date change occurs on a weekend, when demand for electricity is typically lower. The excess generating capacity will mean that if there are problems in one area, there would be excess power available to divert from another area.

Edison Electric Institute's 1998 statement helps to dispel any doom and gloom:

> *More than 96 percent of electrical systems (including 100 percent of operational nuclear reactors) in North America are participating in industry-wide readiness assessments. Efforts will continue toward universal participation.*

> *"Most electrical systems necessary to oper-*
> *ate into the year 2000 will have been tested,*
> *remediated, and will be Y2K Ready by June*
> *30, 1999. Facilities that will miss the June*
> *30, 1999 target are already identified, few in*
> *number, and will not affect electric reliabili-*
> *ty into the year 2000."* [43]

The electric industry has worked for years to plan for Y2K.

Within the electric utility industry, there are hundreds of thousands of computers and software programs that are being checked for Y2K readiness. There are also millions of individual computer chips within critical equipment that are not easily seen or accessible. These are known as 'embedded chips,' which are used in digital controls. These are also being checked.

Electrical systems, however, consist mainly of wires and metal devices. And the majority of equipment is electromechanical, meaning there are no digital controls. In general, electric generation systems are most vulnerable to Y2K, while transmission and distribution systems are less automated and less likely to fail.

Electric utilities do use computer technology for voice and data communications, as well as for monitoring and controlling power systems. Computers help manage purchasing operations, accounting functions, and customer billing and service; and providing for common services such as telephones, security systems, and building elevators. However, some of these functions, like accounting and billing, are not critical to delivering power. And there are definitely accounting software programs available that can correct the problems.

In addition, many of those operations that do rely on computer systems can be manually operated in emergencies - and often are during power outages arising from storms or mechanical problems.

The industry is working to sustain safe and reliable operations during the Y2K transition period. COM/Electric, one of the largest suppliers of electricity in the nation, like most other electric companies, assures people, "We are confident that we will be fully compliant regarding all Year 2000 issues and will continue to provide uninterrupted electricity and related services through the millennium change."

Having electricity available to all of us is of utmost importance. Companies are working hard to correct any problems, so they can fulfill their promise of "uninterrupted service."

Pete Holtzmann, president of the International Christian Technologists'

Association, believes that electric companies are working successfully to fulfill their promise of uninterrupted service. He says, "...Many people are clearly overreacting to the problem. For example, many fear widespread blackouts, even though there is little chance that power delivery, anywhere in the world, will be seriously affected by Y2K." [44]

"U.S. Energy Secretary Bill Richardson said the nation won't experience electrical brownouts on New Year's Day 2000 due to computer problems at utilities. I am confident that there will be no power failures with small power companies (or) big power companies. Our electricity grid is in good shape to meet this (computer) challenge." [45]

If Mr. Richardson's credibility is not very high, it's no surprise. He is one of those most responsible for letting Chinese scientists spy on our nuclear power plants and give or sell priceless technical information to China. Many of the demagogues point to Administration dishonesty when selling their over priced books and tapes.

Nuclear power plants have been designed from the beginning so that they can be shut down manually should there be any safety problems. According to the Edison Electric Institute, "No nuclear facility has found a Y2K problem that would prevent safety systems from shutting down a plant in an emergency. Y2K problems at nuclear facilities do not represent a public health and safety issue." [46]

In testimony before Congress, the NRC (Nuclear Regulatory Commission) reports, "Most nuclear plant safety systems use analog equipment which is not susceptible to the Y2K problem." [47]

"After releasing a report on the state of the electricity industry's preparations for the Year 2000 problem, the North American Electricity Reliability Council is backing up the Nuclear Energy Institute's claims that the nuclear power plants of the US are by and large ready for the millennial date change.

NATIONAL DEFENSE

Despite earlier reports (still being repeated by various speakers and authors), the Department of Defense is ready. Many people are worried that a computer glitch will accidentally launch a nuclear missile at another country, thereby starting an all-out nuclear war. This cannot happen, because there have always been safeguards and back-ups built into the system to prevent accidental launches. Although computers do guide the missiles once they are launched, it takes two people, each using a special mechanical key, to launch a missile.

"We have established that both weapons systems in the United States and Russia and newly independent states do NOT fire without human intervention. There is not that risk," reports John Koskinen, chairman of the U.S. President's Council on Year 2000 Conversion. [48]

SOCIAL SECURITY

One of the biggest concerns people have is whether there will be a disruption of the payments which 45 million Americans currently receive each month from Social Security or from Supplemental Security Income. For many people, this is their sole source of income, and even a few days' delay could cause real hardship.

Every indication is that the Social Security Administration has worked successfully to ensure that they will be ready and that there will be no disruptions in delivery of payments, either by mail or by direct deposit to banks.

The Social Security Administration, like most other government agencies, has hired an independent contractor to check their readiness for the Year 2000 date change. According to Commissioner Fred Apfel, "Both congressional committees and the General Accounting Office have given SSA high marks in its year 2000 efforts, often referring to the Agency as the leader in the federal sector." [49]

Delivery of the payments which millions of people depend upon will not be disrupted. Anarchy will not spill over onto the streets because of people not having their payments.

"Kathy Adams, the Social Security Administration's assistant deputy commissioner for systems, said it took 2,800 workers, including 700 programmers, to ensure the agency's computers are ready for the year 2000.'" [50]

FOOD SUPPLIES

Grocers say there is no need to hoard food for Y2K. As reported by Reuters, "Grocery stores, food makers and a bipartisan group of senators said the Y2K computer problem will not cause disruptions in food supplies and services and urged Americans to refrain from stockpiling. 'This is not a time for people to go crazy or be alarmist,' said Senator Christopher Dodd of Connecticut. 'We see nothing that would cause anyone to want to stockpile large amounts of food.' News reports about soaring sales of dried food and military-style meal kits 'have begun to unnerve many people,' added Dodd, a member of a subcommittee of the Special Senate Committee on the Year 2000 Technology Problem that has been investigating the impact of the 'millennium bug' on various U.S. industries."

"U.S. grocery store chains are spending an average

of $27 million to prepare computers and most expect to have systems installed by mid-summer, according to Tim Hammond, head of the Food Marketing Institute, which represents grocery stores."

"'At this point, we're not seeing anything out of the norm,' said Michael Heschel, executive vice president of Kroger Co., the nation's biggest grocery chain with stores in 31 states. The company plans Y2K tests at Kroger stores this summer to make sure they are ready, he added." [51]

The actual production of food crops depends upon such things as sunshine and rainfall, not computers. The food processing machinery is not going to fail because of a computer chip. In transportation, the trucks are driven by live human beings, who do not necessarily need a computer to tell them where to go. Train transportation may present the greatest problems, but the train tracking system has already been in a mess for years.

BANKING AND INVESTMENTS

"Regulators say nearly 95% of federally insured institutions are making 'satisfactory progress' in readying their computers for the year 2000." [52]

The financial community has been on top of the Y2K computer problem for years. In fact, they were the first to take note of the glitch when they began computations for thirty-year mortgages. Recent transaction tests have proven 100 percent successful.

More recently, they have been issuing Certificates of Deposit that mature in the next century, and have had to make sure their computers can handle them.

100 percent transaction tests of both mortgages and CD's have proven 100 percent successful.

"FDIC insured banks and savings associations are taking steps to make sure their systems will operate smoothly in the Year 2000." [53]

It is estimated that Chase Manhattan Bank in New York has spent over $250 million to correct their millions of lines of codes.

"Several banking companies, including Nations Bank, First Union Corp. And Wachovia Corp., have already spent tens of millions of dollars rewriting and replacing computer software and making other changes."

"For more than a year, they've been checking everything from ATM's and climate-control devices to the time locks on their vaults." [54]

According to banks, Y2K will be okay!

Should individuals withdraw all their money from banks late this year because of the Year 2000 computer problem?

"Banking industry representatives told reporters... that massive withdrawals would be 'foolish,' citing the risk of theft, fire and the interest earnings foregone."

"Banks argue that they will be ready for the date change, citing their consistent rating by experts as among the top industries in preparedness and their existing contingency plans for floods, hurricanes and fires. Automatic teller machines, credit card purchases and direct deposits to bank accounts from employers and social security will continue to work in nearly all cases, they said. 'No one is suggesting there won't be sporadic problems, but they will be isolated,' said Michael Zucchini, chief technology officer at First Financial Group." [55]

First Union advertises on the front cover of their Y2K brochure, "UNLIKE SOME, WE'RE LOOKING FORWARD TO THE YEAR 2000." They continue to say, "At First Union, we're adopting measures to handle all the issues, which means we can look ahead to the new millennium with confidence. First Union has been addressing the subject of Year 2000 since February 1996."

EFT (Electronic Funds Transfers) will not be affected, as test results have proven successful for over one year, according to Mr. Carl Gambs, Fed's Century Date Change Project.

"Y2K will be a nonevent. I am not planning to take my money out," says Cheryl Kane, Bank of America executive vice president of technology. [56]

Anticipating that many people are going to panic anyway, the Federal Reserve has planned on distributing one hundred billion dollars or more in cash to the country's banks. This will insure that banks have sufficient cash on hand in the event people try to withdraw and hoard money. The greatest danger to the banking system will be from a run on the banks, not from computer problems. It would be prudent to have a paper copy of all banking records and a few days supply of cash on hand, but that holds true for any time, not just January 1, 2000.

Edward Kelley, Federal Reserve Board governor, says, "A great deal of very sophisticated and effective work is being done to try to ensure it (Y2K) will not be a disaster." This comment was made in 1998, even before great strides were made to eliminate the problem.

"The consensus of economists in the U. S. is that overall impact on the gross domestic product of the U.S. will only be two-tenths or three-tenths of a percent and they saw no risk of a local or worldwide recession or depression resulting from this,' said John Koskinen, chairman of the U.S. President's Council on Year 2000 Conversion." [57]

CREDIT CARDS

Credit card terminals are Y2K ready. VISA International, Inc., says, "99.4 percent of merchant's credit-card terminals worldwide have been updated to accept cards with expiration dates beyond December 31 (1999). Visa has been helping its 15 million merchants create back-up plans. Those include using hand-operated, carbon-paper credit card processing devices and phoning in transactions if electrical power goes down, rendering electronic terminals useless." [58]

"...(MYTH) People originally screamed that the global credit card system was doomed. (REALITY) Today, the problem has been solved—-45% of all credit cards now have expiration dates after 2000."[59]

The credit card machines of the Religious Freedom Coalition were tested by our bank in 1995 to make sure we were Y2K compliant. We process cards every day that have expiration dates in the year 2000 and the year 2001.

INSURANCE

Insurance is not a problem either.

Prudential, one of America's largest insurance companies with assets over $200 billion, set the pace for other insurance companies to be Y2K compliant.

"For us at Prudential, and for any organization that plans to succeed into the 21st century, failure is not an option. Because we at Prudential have zero tolerance for Y2K failure within our own organization, we have zero tolerance for Y2K failure within any of our business partners' organizations. We are aggressively working with all our partners...'" [60]

INVESTMENTS

Investments are safe. The securities industry continues to test for Y2K problems, surpassing expectations. "More than 400 U.S. securities firms, stock exchanges and asset managers tested this weekend how well their computers will handle stock, bond and mutual fund trades at yearend, when the so-called Year 2000 software problems arise. The test, the first of six on weekends during March and April, went 'better than expected,' according to the Securities Industry Association.... The test included 170,000 transactions for stocks, funds, options and corporate, government, municipal and mortgage-backed bonds." [61]

"Alan Greenspan testified last week that the banking sector is in good shape. Stock exchange tests have also gone well in the U.S., the U.K. and Europe. The Gartner consulting group estimates that only 10 percent of any computer failures are expected to last more than three days. [62]

Is there a strong possibility that Y2K will cause a crash of financial markets in other countries, sending our own stock market into a tailspin? Fox News reports that "Federal Reserve Chairman Alan Greenspan is not worried that the world's financial markets will come crashing down because of the Year 2000 computer problem." Says Dr. Greenspan, "I know the evening news is going to play it as though we were looking at an asteroid about to hit us," but he is more concerned that "people will become more vulnerable to robbers who see an opportunity to get their hands on real cash." [63]

Dr. George Gillen, Chairman of the Business Department at Oral Roberts University advises that Greenspan should be listened to. He says, "Dr. Greenspan, who is perhaps one of the leading economists of our time, has assured us that the best evidence is there is no need for panic. He is the one who has stabilized our economy to the extent that we have on the strongest economies in history. There may be some short-term misallocation of resources, but there is no need for concern. This idea is shared by most leading economists." [64]

"Corporate America is 'in very good shape' to deal with the millennium bug and there is no need to stockpile food or head for the hills come December 31, the top U.S. stock regulator said on Saturday. U.S. Securities and Exchange Commission Chairman Arthur Levitt was asked at a town hall forum in Miami to rate U.S. corporate preparedness to deal with the year 2000 computer bug. On a scale of one to ten, with one being excellent and ten representing 'head for the hills,' Levitt said, 'I'd pick one. I really think we're in very good shape.'"

"Levitt said, 'Corporate America by and large is doing a good job of protecting against Y2K. I think that in the United States, the major companies have spent the money, the time, to protect us.... There is no need for Y2K panic.'" [65]

"It's (Y2K) going to be a dud...we're going to wake up and nothing will have happened," says David Starr, former technology officer at General Motors, ITT and Citicorp in his book "Y2K-666?". [66]

What about the prospect of computers in other countries malfunctioning and causing chaos in our own markets? That is highly unlikely. Doomsayer Michael Hyatt, author of *The Millennium Bug,* predicted such a world wide disaster would actually occur on January 1, 1999. Here is what he said: "The second little secret you need to know about is known as the 'Code 99 Computer Shutdown Secret.' This is the unsolved problem concerning computers that are programmed to interpret the digits 99 as meaning 'cease all computer functions.'....This means that without warning, many of the world's mainframe computers are simply going to shut themselves off on January 1, 1999....Which computers? It doesn't much matter. There is such massive data exchange, also it takes is one computer to corrupt the entire financial information system." [67]

Did anything like this really happen in January of 1999? No, it didn't, and since January the stock market has hit a new record high. Of course something else may send the stock market into a tumble, but it won't be because of Y2K computer problems.

OIL AND GAS

Oil and gas will continue to flow and be distributed in the year 2000.

"The natural gas industry is diligently executing plans to eliminate or deal with operating problems that could arise if computer-based systems do not properly manage the roll-over into the new millennium. This collaborative Y2K effort is an outstanding example of how the various segments of our industry can work together to provide improved energy service with unquestioned reliability," says Steve Ban, GRI President and CEO. [68]

A December 21, 1998 joint press release from the Natural Gas Council and the American Petroleum Institute stated:

> *"The oil and natural gas industries have every reason to believe they will successfully resolve any mission-critical Y2K issues and will continue to deliver oil and natural gas safely and reliably, officials said today."*

> *"Almost all - 94 percent - indicated they will be 'Y2K Ready' by September 30, 1999. As of January, 1999, more than four-fifths of the combined oil and gas industry companies, 86 percent, are in the final stages of fixing and testing business information systems to accommodate the Y2K date. That compares with 55 percent of the companies in the September 1998 survey."*

"As for the embedded hardware systems that must be corrected, 78 percent of respondents said they are in the final stages of fixing and testing hardware and embedded systems for their operational integrity. The response in the September 1998 survey was 46 percent. Nearly all respondents, 97 percent, said they expect to have their Y2K contingency plans in place and tested by the end of the third quarter." (February 18, 1999)

FEDERAL AGENCIES

Federal agencies including, unfortunately, the Internal Revenue Service will continue to operate. The government has apparently passed their first real-world Year 2000 test with flying colors.

"Unemployment insurance benefits claims filed on January 4 have been properly and timely processed by all

50 states, Washington, D.C., and Puerto Rico, according to John Starkey, chief of the IT division for unemployment insurance at the Department of Labor.

"Benefits claims processing was vulnerable to year 2000 problems on January 4, the first business day of the new year, because the claims expire 12 months later, forcing systems to deal with dates in 2000."

"'We got a clean report' Tuesday night from all regional offices," Sharkey said. "No one needed to resort to a contingency plan," he added. [69]

The Government Y2K Task Force issued their interim report on Tuesday, March 2, 1999. Senator Robert Bennett reported that Y2K, "will not be the end of the world as we know it! (a little more optimistic than his original pronouncements) We do not expect that this country (the United States) will be crippled to the point where there will be disastrous consequences over a long period of time." [70]

Added Senator Christopher Dodd, "We have tried to discount the Y2K survivalist's mentality, somehow, that this (Y2K) is going to be Armageddon." [71]

COMMUNICATIONS

Telephone service is expected to continue. "In a report published yesterday, a consortium of major local service providers stated that it expects local telephone service 'to continue without major disruption' throughout the millennium rollover." [72]

Insuring reliable telephone communication into the year 2000 is paramount to every phone provider. Positive results have come from massive testing of phone systems.

Michael Powell, Federal Communications Commissioner, states, "Telephone equipment manufacturers are already producing software that will function properly in the year 2000, enabling phone carriers to meet their own deadlines." [73]

Will you be able to phone home? "Probably," says Michael Powell again. "The biggest threat to the phone system is that everyone will pick up the phone on millennium morn to see if there is a dial tone. That alone could crash the system on any morning. As long as that doesn't happen, Powell is confident that the big telephone companies will be ready." [74]

Again, if you do what you would do normally, there will not be any telephone problems. Don't listen to the scare tactics of the survivalists and demagogues.

Will we get the news about those who took off for the mountains with their dried food?

Yes! "Associated Press' technology is in good shape for the Year 2000. Most of our technology, developed in the past few years, uses all four digits to keep track of the year. Therefore, we have few problems with the two-digit operations of older technology. Over the past few months we have completed testing based on generally accepted industry standard guidelines for Year 2000 (Y2K) compliance." [75]

AIRLINE TRAVEL

The airlines have just had to face the fact that January 1, 2000 will be a low revenue day, no matter what they do or say. "U.S. airlines have been working hard to find and correct any and all problems. Airplanes will not be falling out of the sky. There may be some delays, especially in international travel. Massive work is in progress to make sure that every international airport will continue to function properly." [76]

Boeing, the nation's largest aircraft builder, asserts, "No flight critical effects exist, and safety of flight is not compromised. Normal functionality of the FMS (Flight Management System) is available.

"Boeing plans to be Y2K ready by the end of this calendar year (1998). When the calendar year flips to January 1, 2000, we will be ready." [77]

The FAA passed every part of their simulated early April, 1999 test in reference to landings and takeoffs. "The air-traffic control system, while initially behind, seems to be on schedule to meet the millennium without crisis." [78]

DOCTORS AND HOSPITALS

The medical profession with its over 6,000 hospitals, received the lowest marks from the March 2, 1999 Congressional interim report. However, with the threat of hundreds of millions of dollars in possible lawsuits, there is a very large incentive to be totally Y2K compliant.

In short, the Y2K computer problem is being fixed in a combined effort among every single industry.

8

Y2K May Even Have Some Benefits

CHAPTER 8

Strange as it may seem, there may even be some good things coming forth from the Y2K problem. It has forced countless businesses to modernize their equipment, thereby becoming more efficient and more competitive. Money has poured into the economy; the computer and software industries have hit a bonanza, and all the thousands of people they employ can in turn boost the economy. Y2K has been the spur to discovering new knowledge in computer technology and other fields.

Says James Kudlow in a thought-provoking editorial of March 1999, "Actually, I am now starting to think that the ultimate effects of Y2K will be beneficial to the U. S. economy." [79]

Kudlow goes on to explain that this idea first came to him as he was reading a recent report by Hudson Institute economist Alan Reynolds who had calculated that in 1998, information technology accounted for 41.7 percent of all spending on plants and equipment. It seems logical that some part of this big expenditure for computer hardware and software (probably a large part of it) is due to spending by businesses who have been forced to modernize their systems to get ready for Y2K.

Businesses have been forced to get rid of or upgrade their old, out-of-date computer systems, so now they will be even more efficient and better able to compete in the world markets.

"In sum, Y2K is OK. The Y2K process will prove to be a healthy influence on the economy.... Both industries and interest rates will churn during this new round of technologically induced restructuring, but the net effect will be an inflation-less U.S. economy eve better positioned for value-added wealth creation." [80]

The Y2K problem all revolves around money. A Microsoft programmer spoke to us about what was going on in his industry, but wished to remain anonymous. He said:

> *"A lot of people are on the wrong side of this Y2K issue. The bottom line is, people that are in the moneymaking business are not going to allow something to hinder that money flow if possible. Big companies are replacing equipment and upgrading software. They would rather spend a little now, than lose a lot later. There should be no worries about Y2K because all it is going to*

do is make computer hardware companies richer, as well as the computer software giants like Microsoft. That will be the largest effect of Y2K — the exchange of money; and it has already started. The light, food, etc. will not run short."

When a formerly pessimistic Senator Christopher Dodd confesses, "We're discouraging people from going out and stockpiling," note should be taken. [81]

Others are also trying to eliminate the gloom:

"The infrastructure of the country will hold," says John Koskinen, chairman of the President's Council on Year 2000 Conversion. He added, "...we do not believe there are going to be disruptions related to the year 2000 problem on a national scale." [82]

".... The year 2000 computer problem will be a nonevent," says Sally Katzen, Administrator of U.S. Office of Management and Budget. [83]

"The worst consequence of Y2K will be the result of panic. Companies are providing a resolution. God is in control; and He will

bring His children through," says a much sought-after Christian systems designer who wishes to remain anonymous.

U.S. Senator Robert Bennett (R-UT) finally admitted in early 1999,"In this country, we will have a bump in the road, but it will not be crippling." Senator Bennett had been the sole doomsayer voice in the Congress. Now even he is confident that no real crisis exists outside of the minds of those selling doom for profit.

There are literally hundreds of inexpensive software programs that one can buy at your computer store or Office Depot; or even direct from your computer hardware company. Around Christmas, 1998, Microsoft first offered a tools package to help plan and execute Year 2000 conversion programs, "Now it is action time, to take care of the problem," states Don Jones, Y2K product manager for Microsoft. [84]

The DotComCorp is providing free Y2K bug test software to check individual PC's. *PCNOVICE* has published a *Guide To Y2K* which offers such articles as "How to Identify and Fix Any Year 2000 Problem," which gives simple, do-it-yourself Y2K checks.

Just some of the Y2K programs available for computer users to correct Y2K problems are: PCfix 2000 software from The About Time Group; CentaMeter 2.8 from

Tally Systems Corp.; ZAC 2001 from Network Associates, Inc.; Ezfix; Y2K Sniff; etc. The very big business of fixing Y2K continues to grow! Y2K consultants charge astronomical prices. Thousands of programmers are working around the clock earning huge bucks.

With all the hundreds of millions of lines of computer language that has to be gone through for correction, time was originally thought to be against everyone. But many solutions have been made to literally "fix" the Y2K problem in an automated manner. Many are brand new fixes that actually work. Some are still being tested, but the initial indications are overwhelming.

"Automated software tools have been developed to locate dates. Some of the more advanced products deploy deductive reasoning to achieve astounding rates of success," according to *Scientific American.* [85]

There have been three Y2K date-fixing techniques that are already in widespread use: date expansion, windowing and encapsulation.

"In the early 1990's many experts asserted that date expansion was the best way to tackle Y2K. But the unexpected necessity of having to recompile every program that refers to a date in any file, even when the application does not perform date calculations, has made this approach too expensive and time-consuming for most companies.

"An alternative solution is to teach computers that 00 means 2000. Programmers have extended this simple idea into a strategy called 'windowing'. They have taken all the years from 00 to 99 and divided them into two groups based on a carefully selected pivot (45, for example). Two-digit years greater than or equal to that number are considered to reside in the current century (68 becomes 1968). Everything else is considered to lie in the 21st century (13 becomes 2013).

"Using this concept, a programmer can delve into the source code, find all date references and modify accordingly the calculations involving that information. Because the actual two-digit years themselves do not need to be altered (just the calculations involving those dates are adjusted to place years in the appropriate centuries), windowing requires less work than date expansion and is currently the technique most commonly used to fix Y2K.

"Encapsulation" can be used to sidestep many Y2K problems...the technique becomes unwieldy for complex computations.

"The three techniques—-date expansion, windowing and encapsulation—-have thus far accounted for more than 95 percent of Y2K fixes to existing software." 86

Wayne Rash, Technology Editor of InternetWeek magazine, tells us, "There are several packages available to programmers that do (drastically cut down the time). They all seem to work in different environments. The first was aimed at COBOL on IBM mainframes." [87]

One of the new-breed of exciting solutions to the Y2K problem was invented by StepWise Solutions.

StepWise says this about their innovative program:

> *"StepWise Solutions has the only patented, fully-automated solution for assisting companies with remediation of their computer systems to be Year 2000 compliant. Our patent was granted in September, 1997. We completed the development of our product in June of 1998.*
>
> *"Due to the fully-automated nature of the StepWise Solution, the time necessary to complete remediation of existing code is reduced by an estimated 70% or more."* [88]

Information furnished by StepWise indicates their software can examine software at a rate of four million lines per hour! Michael Hyatt and the other doom salesman never mention StepWise or the other companies mentioned above. They don't want Christians to be alerted to solutions; they only want to "alert" them to dangers.

As Steve Hewitt said, "Six months ago you could talk about how much code the Social Security has to do; but then you look at a new program that Citibank is using, for example, just three months ago, that they are saying now does 30 days work in one day. And that's continuing. Oracle's now coming out with new software that's 100 times faster than that. Companies that are only 25 percent into the embedded chip and into the studies of that, are starting to discover that the damage here is not that bad." [89]

There has been so much talk about "embedded chips." Embedded systems were actually designed by human beings as a part of engineering drawings or computer programs.

"In addition to problems in the computer itself, the Y2K problem also revolves around 'embedded chips.' These are hardware—-miniscule microchips—-holding an incredible amount of information. Among the myriad bits of information imbedded are numerous dates. And these chips appear everywhere. Because embedded chips are so common, it's easy to forget their pervasive presence in our lives." [90]

According to expert Pete Holzmann, "Doomsayers talk about scary 'embedded systems' problem, where an unknown quantity of tiny, hidden computers worldwide will fail on 1/1/2000, causing critical facilities to shut down. They say society's infrastructure is doomed unless these systems are all 100% repaired.

"**Reality:** these embedded systems are real, but the problem isn't nearly as bad as described. I'll just mention three key points the doomsayers ignore:

> *"(1) Critical systems are designed to work with some parts broken. They operate all the time in such a condition!*

> *"(2) Embedded systems that deliver services normally don't care about the date! For example, power plants deliver appropriate amounts of power, no matter what day it is.*

> *"(3) Embedded systems problems that do crop up do not require months or years of repair work, normally they can be reset in seconds, or replaced in minutes or hours. Critical services normally can be placed under manual control. Also, every 'embedded system' critical failure I've ever seen can be readily solved through a manual reset/reboot. These solutions take seconds, minutes or hours, not weeks."* [91]

"*Embedded systems will have limited effect*

> *on Year 2000 problems, and we will see a*
> *minimal number of failures from these*
> *devices. Only one in 100,000 free-standing*
> *micro-controller chips is likely to fail due to*
> *Year 2000."* [92]

There are estimates that the number of embedded chips worldwide is between 32 billion and 40 billion. But do the dates really make a difference, as some of the doom salesmen claim? In some areas. Particularly in the medical field, dates can be important as is illustrated below:

> *"Of course, most of these systems do not*
> *depend on any knowledge of dates and will*
> *therefore not be affected by Y2K. Of those*
> *that are date-sensitive, only a very tiny frac-*
> *tion will suffer anomalous processing.*
> *Nevertheless, even that minute percentage is*
> *still cause for concern. Although nobody*
> *knows for sure the exact number, Gartner*
> *estimates that millions of those embedded*
> *systems are vulnerable.*
>
> *"A common solution is to make one-for-one*
> *replacements of the offending chips, includ-*

ing real-time clocks (which keep track of time with a crystal oscillator) and micro-processors and controllers (which instruct a device to perform certain actions). The process might be as simple as pulling the parts off printed circuit boards and plugging in their newer counterparts that are inscribed with revised software designed to handle Y2K. Often, though, the entire piece of equipment must be scrapped and replaced—-obviously an expensive course of action but sometimes a necessary one, par-ticularly if the device will have trouble cal-culating a patient's radiation dosage." [93]

It is for precisely this reason that all essential medical devices are being tested well in advance to make sure they function correctly. Keep in mind, however, that the overwhelming majority of medical devices have no 'date-set' chips. Some X-ray units for example do print a date on the negative (most don't). The lack of an auto date does not affect the outcome of the X-ray.

According to top Christian computer consultant Doug Preudhomme, "99% of embedded systems are 'process control' systems and they have no idea what the date is. Unless there is a way an embedded chip can set the date, then the year is irrelevant. Almost all embedded systems do not have any date-set structure." [94]

One company has come up with the "Delta-T Probe." It is a unique non-invasive diagnostic tool which attaches to and monitors chips with the embedded system. It is capable of determining whether an embedded system processes date and time at all. But this remarkable device is not the total cure.

"Lots of embedded chips have a date function. The question is what they do with it. Virtually none of these embedded chips have the authority to do anything beyond sounding alarms and logging date problems. They do not have the ability to shut down anything. In many cases, they simply add dates to reports for convenience," reports Wayne Rash, Technology Editor of *InternetWeek.* [95]

Whether it is searching for billions of embedded chips or overhauling entire systems, new computer technology is coming forth. In the Y2K "race against time," computer scientists are winning the race, thanks to the technological breakthroughs, whether or not they were motivated by the Y2K alert.

No matter what, we are happy to report: "Houston, we do not have a problem!"

Practical Preparation:

Finding a Proper Balance

CHAPTER 9

Each life has joy and sorrow, pleasure and pain. Each new encounter in life must be addressed in a balanced manner and Y2K is no exception. All individuals should take reasonable precautions with Y2K or any other unpredictable event they may encounter. It is most probable that people will neither starve nor freeze to death in January of 2000; however, some computer problems are still likely to occur. For that matter computer glitches, weather problems or illness can cause families problems at any time.

In any emergency the Red Cross stands out as an organization ready to help those in need. It is also the largest supplier of blood to hospitals in the United States. The Red Cross as an organization will be Y2K compliant and is working with its suppliers to make sure they are as well. The Red Cross Internet site makes very clear their current condition as far as Y2K readiness:

"The Information Systems Division at national headquarters is in the process of ensuring that all national headquarters-supported software used by national headquarters, chapters, Blood Services regions, and other units is Year 2000 compliant. In addition, the Year 2000 Project Office is actively gathering information on our suppliers' Year 2000 compliance status. We are developing contingency plans to prevent our supply chain from being adversely affected by the Year 2000. Our lines of service, Biomedical Services, Chapter Services, and Disaster Services also have Year 2000 readiness activities underway throughout the organization." [96]

The Red Cross has also issued guidelines for the Y2K event that are the same as those for tornadoes, winter storms and family illness. The Red Cross recommends that everyone should have a least seven days of food at home at all times, not just for Y2K. Every family should have enough food on hand to get through a bad case of flu without going to the grocery store. Homes should always have candles and battery operated radios in case of storms.

In a statement the Red Cross defended its recommendation to have food and water in the home for Y2K:

"Red Cross recommendations to have food, water, and other emergency supplies on hand are not new, and are considered reasonable in case of any disaster. Our recommendations are to have supplies to last at least three days to a week. Most reasonable people would not consider such quantities of supplies as a "stockpile" or "hoarding." We understand that there are some other groups or organizations that are suggesting storing larger quantities of

supplies for various reasons. We will stick with our recommendations, because experience with hundreds of disasters over many, many years has indicated that the vast
majority of people in the U.S. can get to one of our shel-
ters for caring comfort or receive other assistance in a matter of a few days after even the most severe event." [97]

As the Red Cross points out in all its literature, it is
also prudent to be prepared for an emergency and that
includes always maintaining duplicates of important docu-
ments such as bank and social security records. In the Red
Cross manual, *Y2K What You Should Know*, recommendations include having at least half a tank of gas in your car,
up to a one week supply of food and the same amount of
cash you would have on hand should there be a snow
storm. The Red Cross also recommends changing the batteries in fire alarms, even the backup batteries in those that
are hard wired. This is something that should be done year-
ly anyway. Much of the Red Cross Y2K manual tells what
not to do. They advise, for example, not to run generators
or camp stoves indoors. All this information is available at
the Red Cross Internet site at: www.redcross.org.

Y2K preparedness should include:

1. *Copies of insurance, investment, house
   payment and credit card records.*

2. *A normal week's supply of food.*

3. *At least half a tank of gas in each car.*

3. *A normal weekend supply of cash.*

4. *Some extra batteries and a battery-oper-ated radio*

5. *Stay informed!*

Although we, the authors, do not believe there will be any major interruption in the flow of power or natural gas because of computer failure in the United States, problems could arise because of crime. Dissemination of vital information is paramount. There is a wealth of information available from reliable sources. Unfortunately many of the "doom" sites come up when searching for information on the Internet.

There is, for example, a Y2K database available on the Internet individuals can check to find out if their supplies of fuel, power and water are indeed Y2K compliant. The data base can be accessed at www.Y2Kbase.com. There is a built-in search engine that can be used to locate infor-mation on the compliance of local phone companies and utilities. For even greater details on utilities the Edison Electric Institute can be contacted. The Edison Internet site located at www.eei.org will put even the most skeptical minds at ease about the power supply in the year 2000.

If there is a power failure or other problems caused by

panic or riots, it is a surety that the left-leaning media will blame it on conservative preachers. Unfortunately, some preachers have already predicted starvation and general gloom, as previously mentioned. It is shameful that these few pastors and prophets of doom will adversely affect the general public's perception of all clergy.

It should be no pastor's desire to cause a panic. There are positive voices from the conservative, evangelical community beside those of the authors.

Beverly LaHaye says, "Faith – rather than fear – should be the Christian response (to Y2K)!" [98]

We whole-heartedly agree with noted author Dr. David Shibley who writes: "Take my advice, don't head for the hills! The last thing we need in the church today is a wave of hysteria.

"I couldn't believe it!" says Shibley, "A noted speaker (Christian) recently announced he was redirecting his entire ministry to help Christians prepare for the potential fallout associated with Y2K. This brother is convinced he is doing something noble. But my first reaction was, 'What a pathetic way to spend the next fourteen months!'

"Here we are in the most colossal harvest in 20 centuries, and the energies of thousands of believers are being diverted by mild hysteria over Y2K. Hey, get over it! All this panic is creating paralysis and a blurred focus.

"Certainly there is a biblical case for taking precautionary measures. But the 'head for the hills' phobia that is engulfing many would be amusing if it weren't so dangerous. The 'Y2K blues' is a serious, contagious illness that drains energy and makes us lose sight of the Great Commission.

"We cannot allow the world system or calamities — real or imagined — to set our agenda. Our agenda has been set by Jesus Himself: Go and make disciples of all nations! We have no authorization to pre-empt His top priority. I don't want to spend the next year preparing the church for Y2K. I want to spend this time preparing the church for the coming of the Lord...Stay focused. Don't be diverted by lesser agendas." [99]

Although there are voices such as that of Dr. Shibley's, there are far too many others leading people astray. Let us not forget the Hale-Boop Comet incident in 1997. Thirty-nine people committed suicide expecting their spirits to be lifted up into a spacecraft in the tail of the comet. We look back with sorrow at these lost lives and lost souls. The left-leaning news media will bring comparison after comparison of that ill-fated Heavens Gate cult with Christian survivalists. And there may very well be some actual suicides on New Years' Eve among those who have been convinced the end of the world is at hand. Christians will be made to look as foolish and as pathetic as those who followed cult leader Marshall

Applewhite on his ill-fated journey to Hale-Boop.

> *"But know this, that in the last days perilous times will come."*
>
> — *2 Timothy 3:1*

As the year 2000 creeps even closer, survivalists and millennialist cults are becoming ever more frenzied. Despite Y2K problems being fixed every day, many of them are still convinced that the world will end on or soon after January 1, 2000.

Many corporate information management officers are now speaking out about Y2K: "As an MIS manager, I'm getting really tired of people who are hyping the dark side of the Y2K issue.

"These fearmongers are either outright kooks who are latching onto the current fear of the day or shrewd profiteers akin to mail and phone scammers. They want to create an environment in which their dire predictions become self-fulfilling.

"I don't want to trivialize the situation—-there will be some issues. Common sense, rational thinking and testing will help solve this problem. On the other hand, the worst-case scenario would have made one hell of a 'Twilight Zone' episode," reports MIS manager Bert J. Bingel. [100]

Life will go on as God intended it to! On January 1,

on January 2 and on January 3 the doomsayers will be proven wrong again. "Damage control" among Christian groups will be similar to the "spin" at the White House during the Monica affair. Liberal publications such as *TIME* magazine and the *WASHINGTON POST* will have a field day writing stories about "Christian Y2K survivalists" coming back from the hills. CNN probably already has plans to shoot footage of the more bazaar cases coming out of their foxholes. The cause of Christ will be damaged because the credibility of Christians throughout America will have been damaged by hysteria and fear.

> *"For God has not given us a spirit of fear,*
> *but of power and love and of sound mind."*
> — *2 Timothy 1:7*

Those who fear the future on Earth have not placed their eternal trust in God. He is our protector, He is our Provider.

There are Christian leaders who warn against hoarding and for good biblical reason. Even when we do store food it should not be out of fear, but rather only as God's word would tell us. Doug Heil, president of the International Leadership Training Institute in Columbus, Ohio said: "If a person's motivation to lay up provisions is based on good stewardship principles, not on fear, then there is nothing wrong with storing up for the lean times. (God warned Egypt they would have seven good years then seven bad years). If a Christian's primary motivation for creating a larder is fear, they are trusting in their own ability to stave off the devourer, and all their efforts will come to naught." [101]

As Christians, we must always be ready for the Lord's return, but not at the expense of causing fear and panic among people. Let us take to heart the following scriptures.

"The prudent sees the evil and hides himself, but the naive go on, and are punished for it."
> — *Proverbs 22:3*

"A prudent man foreseeth the evil, and hideth himself; but the simple pass on, and are punished."
> — *Proverbs 27:12*

"For yourselves know perfectly that the day of the Lord so cometh as a thief in the night."
> — *I Thessalonians 5:2*

"But the day of the Lord will come as a thief in the night; in the which the heavens shall pass away with a great noise, and the elements shall melt with fervent heat, the earth also and the works that are

therein shall be burned up."

— *2 Peter 3:10*

"Therefore be ye also ready: for in such an hour as ye think not the Son of man cometh."

— *Matthew 24:44*

"Be ye therefore ready also: for the Son of man cometh at an hour when ye think not."

— *Luke 12:40*

RELIGION TODAY carried an article of interest, which shows how Y2K panic-struck Christians in America are viewed by that part of the world that is suffering from starvation:

"Jim Jacobson is concerned about American Christians. And he's angry. Jacobson, president of Christian Freedom International, has seen dreadful persecution in Sudan and Burma. But back home in Texas and Michigan, Christians don't seem to care much about the suffering of their brothers and sisters in Christ - they just want to talk about Y2K."

".... 'I'm frankly floored by it,' Jacobson told RELIGION TODAY. 'When you are around persecuted Christians, then you see people whine and get nervous about this (Y2K)... I have very little empathy about it. Has the church come down to this?'

"Some churches are 'becoming like a militia, stockpiling food and adopting a bunker mentality,' Jacobson said. One congregation ousted its pastor because he was 'not diehard enough' about preparing for Y2K. Another church nearly went through a split because of disagreement over the issue. 'Incredible,' he said.

"... 'There are so many current needs ... where people are doing nothing to help our brothers and sisters, and yet are hoarding for some theoretical event. Shame on the church.' Jacobson finds it disturbing that 'Christians behave like this. There is a real spirit of fear. We are not supposed to have a spirit of fear or be anxious for tomorrow.' Y2K mania is 'almost like an evil plot to paralyze the church.' He said.

"... 'When I go to Third World places they laugh about it. They have nothing——no electricity, no running water. There is nothing but people fighting for their lives. You tell them Christians in the United States are scared to death about a computer problem, and they don't know whether to laugh or cry for us.'

"Jacobson says he understands the potential seriousness of Y2K, and agrees that it is good to be 'prudent and wise.' But even 'if God is going to work through a computer we should not let this get us down as Christians. Rejoice because our redemption draws nigh.'" [102]

The Y2K situation is an indicator that we should be

prepared at all times as the Lord would have us be. Not just prepared for Y2K or weather problems, but for our Salvation and the Salvation of others as well. This is not the time to buy ammo and hide with dried food in the hills like a frightened animal. Y2K is not an excuse to hide; Y2K is a reason to carry boldly forth the banner of Christ for all to see. We should be shameless in Him and cast our lot, our future both here and in Eternity with the Lord.

God has granted us domination over the earth. It is our duty and responsibility to care for our families and the resources given us by God. Ultimately, however, we must trust Him first and not ourselves. If this would be the End Time of God's plan then no human preparation could prepare against it. We must then follow God's Word and be prudent in our storehouse preparations as to not foolishly waste the resources He has given us.

On New Years Eve, 1999 the authors will not be hiding in some remote area of the mountains, but rather expanding the Great Commission, as He commanded us.

The Y2K software problem is not a destroyer, it is an opportunity to tell the world about the real End Time and the real solution to life-on-earth's inevitable end. That solution is a personal relationship with Jesus Christ.

Please, for His sake, stop the madness!

FOOTNOTES

1   Keyes, Benjamin, Ph.D. Personal interview with Bob Armstrong, February 16, 1999.

2   www.icta.net/y2k.

3   www.abcnews.com

4   Ibid.

5   Y2K statements, www.microsoft.org (Internet)

6   W. Kevin Armstrong, Virginia Beach Editor, *THE VIRGINIAN-PILOT,* personal interview, January 28, 1999.

7   www.abcnews.com

8   *KIPLINGER Newsletter,* January, 1999, P. 112.

9   *Bloomberg News,* March 7, 1999

10 Y2K statements, www.microsoft.org (Internet)

11 Ibid.

12 Ibid.

13 "SOFTWARE GLITCH TAKES OUT SCHWAB WEB SITE," *USA TODAY,* February 25, 1999.

14 Hyatt, Michael S. *The Millennium Bug: How to Survive the Coming Chaos,* Regnery Publishing, Washington, D.C., 1998. P 169.

15 Ibid. p. 8.

16 Ibid. p. 175

17 *Y2KCPR* Vol. 1 August, 1998, p. 14.

18 www.garynorth.com/y2k Category: Banking

19 *Reuters News Service,* September 5, 1998.

20 *Gartner Group Report,* October 7, 1998.

21 Dr. Benjamin Keyes, February 16, 1999, interview.

22 Wilkerson, David. *World Challenge, Inc.* newsletter of December 1998.

23   Jeffrey, Dr. Grant. *The Millennium Meltdown.* p. 5.

24   Radio Broadcast, November 10, 1998.

25   Sutton, Dr. Hilton. *Mission to America* newsletter, January, 1999, www.hilton-sutton.org

26   *TIME* magazine, January 18, 1999, pages 60-70.

27   *PC COMPUTING Magazine,* Editorial, February, 1999, by Paul Somerson.

28   Ibid.

29   Ibid.

30   "Don't Believe the Hype," Fred Moody, ABC NEWS.com, August 11, 1998).

31   Ibid.

32   "Separating Fact From Fiction in the Y2K Crisis," *InternetWeek Magazine,* Editorial, January 25, 1999.

33   Ibid.

34   Dan Wooding, *ASSIST Communications,* e-mail, January 18, 1999.

35   "Y2k: What's Really Going to Happen?", ICTA Research Report #1, by Pete Holzmann.

36   Ibid.

37   Steve Hewitt, editor, *Christian Computing Magazine,* as he spoke on an October, 1998 Dr. James Dobson radio broadcast.

38   Ibid.

39   Evangelical Lutheran statement on Y2K, 1998.

40   www.icta www.icta.net/y2k, Pete Holzmann.

41   ABC NEWS Online-September 26, 1998, by Chris Stamper.

42   Edison Electric Institute.

43   Ibid.

44   "Y2k: What's Really Going to Happen?", ICTA Research Report #1, by Pete Holzmann.

45   Ibid.

46   Edison Electric Institute, Annual Report, 1998.

47   "NRC's Year 200 Activities," Nuclear Regulatory Commission Report, November 17, 1998.

48   Reuters News Agency, March 3, 1999.

49   www.socialsecurity.gov, May 6, 1999.

50 Ibid.

51 Vorman, Julie. Reuters News Agency, March 2, 1999.

52 *Kiplinger Newsletter,* January 1999, p. 16.

53 "The Year 2000 Date Change: What It Means to You and Your Insured Financial Institution," FDIC brochure.

54 *THE VIRGINIAN-PILOT,* Business News, July 12, 1998, p. D4.

55 ABCNEWS.com, Reuters, "Banks: Y2K Will Be OK," November 20, 1998.

56 "Debunking Year 2000's Computer Disaster," by Greg Miller, Los Angeles Times, November 3, 1997, p. 1A.

57 Reuters News Agency, March 2, 1999.

58 *Bloomberg News,* March 4, 1999.

59 www.icta.net/y2k, Pete Holzmann.

60 Irene Dec, Prudential's vice president of corporate information; May 7, 1998 House Committee on Ways and Means, Hearing on the Year 2000 Computer Problem.

61 *Bloomberg News,* March 4, 1999.

62 *Gartner Group Report,* October 7, 1998.

63 Fox News, May 1999.

64 Dr. George Gillen, personal interview with Bob Armstrong —

65 CMPnet, "Government Passes First y2k Test,"January 7, 1999.

66 Starr, David. *Y2K-666?,* Hutchings & Spargimino, Hearthstone Publishing, 1998, p. 72.

67 Hyatt, *Y2KCPR* Vol. 1 August 1998, p. 15.

68 "Working Together to Find Solutions," GRID Magazine, Fall, 1998.

69 CMPnet, "Government Passes First Y2K Test," January 7, 1999.

70 United States Senate News Conference, March 2, 1999.

71 Ibid.

72 Tim Wilson, *InternetWeek Newsletter,* March 4, 1999.

73 Reuters News Agency, June 17, 1998.

74 Ibid.

75 Jeffrey A. Hastie, Associated Press Deputy Director, Communications and Technology, June 19, 1998.

76 IATA summary, www.icta.net/y2k (Internet).

77 "Getting Ready for the Millennium," Boeing and the Year 2000 Challenge, June 19, 1998.

78 *Kiplinger Newsletter,* January 1999, p. 112.

79 Kudlow, James. *Bloomberg News,* March 5, 1999.

80 Ibid.

81 *Y2K Task Force Report,* March 2, 1999.

82 www.abcnews.com (Internet).

83 Sally Katzen testimony before Congressional Subcommittee, July 10, 1997.

84 CNET, January 1999.

85 *Scientific American,* January 1999, pages 89-90.

86 Ibid.

87 Rash, Wayne. "Separating Fact from Fiction in theY2K Crisis," *InternetWeek Magazine,* January 25, 1999.

88 www.stepwise.com, November 18, 1998.

89 Steve Hewitt, editor, *Christian Computing Magazine,* as he spoke on an October, 1998 radio broadcast with Dr. James Dobson.

90 "Y2K: End of the world or no big deal?," Jessica Wadkins, *Family Voice,* p. 5.

91 "Y2K: What's Really Going to Happen?" Pete Holzmann, *ICTA Research Report # 1* Fall, 1998.

92 *Gartner Group Report,* October 7, 1998.

93 *Scientific American,* January, 1999, p. 92.

94 Doug Preudhomme, personal E-mail message to Bob Armstrong, January 28, 1999.

95 Rash, Wayne.

96 www.redcross.org, April 16, 1999.

97 Ibid.

98 Beverly LaHaye, *Family Voice,* November/December, 1998.

99 Dr. David Shibley, "Take My Advice: Don't head for the Hills!" *Charisma magazine,* December, 1998.

100 Bert J. Bingel, MIS manager, Ames Textile Corp., Lowell, MA, *InternetWeek,* February 8, 1999, p. 30.

101 Doug Heil, International Leadership Training Institute, Columbus, OH, personal e-mail to author, February 27, 1999.

102 Jacobson, Jim. *Religion Today,* September 18, 1998.